TEACH YOUR BUSINESS TO REJOICE!

Unlock The Supernatural Power Of Communication And Honor

Tyler Frick

Resurgence Media

CONTENTS

INTRODUCTION

Welcome to a journey like no other, where business meets Spirit, and practicality intertwines the supernatural with profound strategies for increase, honor, and dynamic communications. Welcome to "Teach Your Business to REJOICE! - Unlock the Supernatural Power of Communication & Honor"!

This book is not simply another handbook on business tactics or strategies. Instead, it opens an entirely new paradigm, where honor and communication form the bedrock of an authentic and successful organization. I've written this book with a singular aim in mind: to empower you to lead a movement within your business, one that produces flourishing culture through Kingdom values, teaching you to move in the power of honoring each individual's unique gifts and identities, beyond skillset, job roles, and income goals.

"Teach Your Business to REJOICE!" brings the supernatural into the realm of the practical. It reveals the hidden strength of collaboration with the Holy Spirit, prophets, and intentional operations like visionary roundtables. It goes beyond the surface level of business conduct, delving into the depths of pure communication, and a dialogue that speaks of honor, respect, and understanding.

This book will challenge your perception of business leadership. It will push you to the limits of your understanding and comfort, but it will also equip you with the tools and wisdom to make your business an environment where people don't just work - they thrive, they grow, and they rejoice!

As you flip through these pages, I hope that you will discover that the supernatural power of communication and honor is not just a lofty ideal but a tangible, achievable reality, when partnered with the right source of inspiration. The path to this transformation may not be easy, but it promises a reward far greater than you could ever imagine: a thriving, joyful business and a team that creates exceeding potential through the experience of being valued, motivated, and fulfilled. So, are you ready to embrace this new paradigm? Are you prepared to lead a movement in your business? Are you excited to unlock the power of pure communication, to collaborate with the Holy Spirit, and to honor the unique essence of every team member?

Welcome to your journey.

Tyler Frick

CHAPTER ONE: THE POWER OF PURE COMMUNICATION

I want to welcome you to this dynamic journey we're about to embark on together. This book is titled with a unique message, exhortation, and invitation: "Teach your Business to Rejoice!" Throughout each chapter, I'll be taking you into spiritual concepts, principles, and protocols that I believe will activate supernatural growth for your business, leadership endeavors, and more. To begin, we'll delve into the dynamics of "The Power of Pure Communication."

As we move through this chapter, I encourage you to take notes, reflecting on what you're hearing, seeing, and learning. Communication, as we will discover, is a two-way street. It's both receiving and releasing. If you'll commit to opening your heart, as well as your mouth about what you learn in this book, I believe you'll activate a mighty movement of expansion in your life and leadership. I know you just started reading, but go ahead and pause, pray, and make an intentional decision to take this seriously. I'll be sharing some strategic insights that might require you to flip some things upside down to access your inheritance. When you're ready...keep reading. It's about to get EXCITING!!

Our first concept is this: The power truly lies in pure communication. But when I mention power, what does that signify? I'm not talking about mere human might or prowess. I'm not talking about influence, wealth, or the size of your impact. Instead, I refer to a divine power that is purposed in grace to uplift your business, leadership, and life - all stemming from the way you handle communications.

Consider this: What if your business could operate with a supernatural power, a power birthed from your obedience and the way you manage communications with the people you are reaching, leading, or impacting? This power could elevate your business to phenomenal financial heights and broaden its sphere of influence into more dominions, industries, and nations. It can benefit you in every conceivable way. But to harness it, you must understand the power of communication and the power of people.

Approaching people correctly is the key to building trust. Literally, how you approach people with ideas, corrections, insights, and more can regulate the opportunity you host in conversations with every person you speak to. Imagine the revelation I just shared for a moment, and consider the significance of every "approach" you make in conversation and communication with the people around you. The truth is, if you are unsure about how to approach people, you are likely unsure about how to build trust. This connection between communication and trust is a significant conduit for the divine power that will ascend your business.

For some, relating something spiritual to business might seem unusual. However, we share a world, this vast cosmos full of billions of people, in a created space that was fashioned to establish you for greater dominion. It's not too far-fetched to recognize that we're engaging with a spiritual dimension in everything we do. We literally fly around in space on a planet surrounded by an ever-expanding universe that was ignited by the voice of our Creator.

Everything you experience in life is the result of communication. This book will help you understand and approach a healthy pursuit of advancing in life, leadership, and business through the power of both spiritual and practical communications.

The power of pure communication can elevate your business, mainly through the realm of trust. But how do we really define trust? I want you to think of it like a bank, where the presence of people and what they have in their possession generates trust. Mismanaging this trust could limit the potential for mutually beneficial relationships and restrict access to your inheritance.

I firmly believe that each of you have a unique inheritance

waiting to be claimed, and the Father is ready to bestow it. Yet, in order to receive it, though, you must learn to listen. In this journey, I will teach you how to tune in to what God is wanting to do in and through you and what His voice, embodied in the Holy Spirit, is communicating about your potential to access your inheritance through your relationships and how He influences them.

Holy communication forms the foundation of leadership in your business. Do you want to be a leader who functions in the kind of power that changes the lives of everyone who encounters you? Or, would you rather play the role of an influential person who has no impact on people, but can generate a few dollars for the longevity of an enterprise? At some point, if you aspire to succeed, you will need to find boldness, confidence, and determination to rule in your industry with influence that does more than create material increase. If you want to do more than make money and products, consider the fruitfulness that is produced when you step into the light, and out of the darkness.

John 12:44-50, provides some insights;

> "And Jesus cried out and said, "Whoever believes in me, believes not in me but in him who sent me. And whoever sees me sees him who sent me. I have come into the world as light, so that whoever believes in me may not remain in darkness. If anyone hears my words and does not keep them, I do not judge him; for I did not come to judge the world but to save the world. The one who rejects me and does not receive my words has a judge; the word that I have spoken will judge him on the last day. For I have not spoken on my own authority, but the Father who sent me has himself given me a commandment—what to say and what to speak. And I know that his commandment is eternal life. What I say, therefore, I say as the Father has told me."

Jesus explains that whoever believes in Him is, in fact, placing their faith in the One who sent Him. He came as a beacon of light, and was given what to say and what to speak in order that he could provide instruction for fullness of life, so believers need not remain in darkness. Here, darkness signifies not your troubles, but the inability to see correctly.

If you feel like you're operating in the dark, hitting obstacles unexpectedly, know that this can be changed. Even in your own home, walking around at night in the dark can be dangerous, especially when your kids like to play with Legos® and not put them back up! (I'm a father of four boys, and I've experienced the excruciating pain that comes from stepping on Legos® at 3AM!) Jesus declared that He didn't come to judge but to save the world. He's not here to condemn you. His teachings are designed to guide, not to punish.

I understand that not everyone who reads this book will read it from the perspective of a submitted son or daughter of God, so let me just say this. In this first chapter, I will cover a few things from a bit of an evangelistic perspective, then we're moving on to the depth of understanding he's given me to teach you how to lead your business into a position to REJOICE. So, let's get to it.

Whether you accept it or not, Jesus is King. You are a creative being, and God seeks to influence you. He wants to build a relationship with you to unleash a creative design in your business and the world, enabling you to rule alongside the Creator of the universe. This book was birthed in the Secret Place in my time with God. Keep reading even if you don't like that reality, because it will still blow your mind.

Being on the team of the universe's Creator sounds like a winning side, doesn't it? God's not here to pass judgment; He's here to share wisdom, instruction, and hope as he woos us into his presence. He put the punishment on his own Son, Jesus, on the cross so that you could have access to life in the midst of your mess. If the cross wasn't good enough, you would still must earn his love, but that's just not the case. Let's take the opportunity right here in this book to open ourselves up to life and to that wisdom and see how it can transform our businesses and our lives. What do you say?

Ok, so here's the task at hand - the Holy Spirit begins to convict us of righteousness, guiding us to live and operate in a specific way. With Jesus no longer visible on Earth, we rely on the Holy

Spirit to convey His teachings, His righteousness, and His ways of doing things. The Holy Spirit also convicts us about judgment, not necessarily about being judged ourselves, but recognizing that the ruler of this world has already been judged. The voice of the Holy Spirit doesn't lead to condemnation and reminders about how guilty, worthless, or evil you are. In fact, that's what the voice of the devil sounds like. But the devil has no authority, he's just a defeated punk.

Imagine operating under an authority that is above all others, an authority that hasn't and will never be judged as anything other than holy because it's perfect. This book is about accessing this level of authority in your life and your business. When the Holy Spirit comes, He will guide you towards all truth. The truth is a person - Jesus Christ. The Holy Spirit guides you towards Jesus, towards truth, and towards knowing what you need to understand, whether that pertains to the past, present, or future. This is true for you personally, first. However, the conversation that God holds with us through the Spirit doesn't end at personal convictions about life, salvation, etc. It is the vital force that created everything you experience in the first place, including your business, desires, excitement, and opportunities.

Frankly, God is better at business than you. He invented the concept of business, and is the end-all be-all when it comes to achieving success.

The amazing thing about the Holy Spirit's voice is that he doesn't speak on its own authority but is submitted to the authority of the Father. The Bible literally says in John 16, When the Spirit of truth comes, he will guide you into all the truth, for he will not speak on his own authority, but whatever he hears he will speak, and he will declare to you the things that are to come. Hence, there is no need to worry about being led astray. Trust is the pivotal factor here. The Holy Spirit will speak what He hears, influencing your life, business, relationships, and everything else that you're involved with. He will provide guidance, helping you navigate your path with grace, ease, and success.

Whoa. This one reality, when honored, creates endless

opportunities for you. All of those opportunities are powered by the conversation you're willing to have with God through the Holy Spirit. This opportunity isn't reserved for a select few. It's available for everyone willing to receive him, listen to him and allow themselves to be led by the Spirit of God. If you yearn to tap into the power of pure communication, to truly comprehend the potential that lies within you through your ability to communicate and build relationships, you need to connect with the Holy Spirit. He needs to become your best friend, your daily joy, and your most sought-after conversation. That is the key to unlocking the power of pure communication in your life.

When you think about judgment, it's essential to consider what the verse says. Often, we might jump to the conclusion that we're doing everything wrong. We're living in sin, making numerous mistakes, and so we have no other option but to anticipate divine judgment, expecting a heavenly lightning bolt to be thrown down to set us straight. Consequently, through that line of thinking, we feel compelled to become flawless beings to attain salvation. However, that's not the gospel; it's a misconception. It's not the truth. There is indeed a time for righteousness and repentance, but God's approach to us is not based on harsh judgment. If that's what you've been led to believe, then you've been misled.

The verse indicates that the Holy Spirit convicts the world of judgment because the ruler of this world has already been judged. The Holy Spirit speaks more about the enemy's judgment than yours, as your judgment is fundamentally mercy. To approach God, to reach the Father, the only way is through Jesus. That's the truth. I'm here to proclaim this truth, and what you do with it is your choice. Jesus, the King of Kings and Lord of Lords, died on a cross and shed His blood for your salvation. The only thing you need to do is believe in Him. The opportunity is there for you.

Ok... so, who is this ruler of the world? The one who has already been judged? This ruler, the adversary, is Satan. Satan is the one you've probably been contending with when you grapple with discontent, panic attacks, anxiety, and emotional upheaval. When your mind seems chaotic, remember that there's nothing wrong with you; you merely have an adversary. But don't worry, I'll teach you how to deal with him.

Satan is the enemy of God, of all that God does, and all that God loves (including you). He's known as the devil in the New Testament, a term that translates to 'a false accuser.' So, when you feel doubt and insecurity as a leader, the root of these feelings might just be this false accuser, inciting feelings of shame, guilt, rejection, and discord. The problem we're dealing with is this world, this age, and the ruler who seeks to thrive here. However, he has already been judged. There may be a delay in him receiving his punishment, but rest assured, his time is coming. In the Greek language, the words 'cosmos' and 'aion' are used for the same English word "world", and are used to describe both the created world (the entire universe) and the age (the timeline of the world's existence). Cosmos refers to the spiritual and physical world created by God but given up by man. Aion describes this age, an age that is doomed to pass away and has no authority over eternity and eternal truths, realities, powers, or principles. This world, ruled by Satan, has been redeemed by the blood of Jesus and is scheduled to pass away.

We were created as immortal beings, positioned to experience eternity. Our existence will continue for eternity, some of us in holiness, and others in suffering. Even though we all had a beginning, we will have no end. Even after this earth passes away, you won't. The question is, how do you want to spend your eternity? It's a choice we must make. Within the cosmos, 'aion' does not refer to the physical universe but a period of time, an age with a beginning and an end. We operate our businesses within this world, within this age. However, we can have our businesses led from a place of eternity, not constrained by the beginning or the end. God is not bound by time; He is outside of time, which means the ideas, strategies, and guidance He provides us are not restricted by our circumstances. Often we look at our businesses and identify targets we need to reach, thinking that these metrics and goals are the ultimate path forward. Yet there is a divine strategy that may reveal itself making all those meticulous plans and numbers seem nearly irrelevant.

God might provide a plan that seems entirely out of the ordinary, even preposterous at first glance. This plan could involve something that doesn't exist yet which, potentially, you are destined to invent. This may sound unappealing to some, but to most it is an exciting reality that stirs hope and desire to operate in the power of revelation, and I can assure you of its power because I've experienced it. It works, and I am fascinated by it.

Just as eternity has no beginning and no end, God's Word remains forever true, transcending every industry, system, and human-made structure. Romans 12:2 provides guidance for us in this regard, urging us not to conform to this world but be transformed by the renewing of our minds. This principle extends not only to personal life but to every venture you undertake, including building your business. In that verse, the word "world" is not cosmos, but "aion', the age and timeline of our physical existence, but not our spiritual existence.

God's principles cut across all facets of life, transcending every industry, every system, and every sphere of influence. As business owners who lead people, we need to embrace this. There's a spiritual movement currently sweeping across the world, and it prompts us to question whether we want to be a part of it. We need to ask ourselves whether we want to be part of the spiritual awakening unfolding across the globe. In the charismatic Christian world, many are believing for a billion-soul harvest in this hour. Yet most don't realize that this harvest will be stewarded by entrepreneurs and business leaders just as much as pastors and church leaders. Often, we anticipate divine interventions to happen within the walls of our churches. Yet, God's kingdom is not restricted to these establishments. It is broader and richer, extending far beyond the confines of any structure. The local church plays a vital role, yes, but it is not the entirety of the kingdom. God's influence reaches you wherever you are, regardless of your faith or doubts. The Holy Spirit has been speaking to everyone on the earth from birth, guiding, and convicting us to follow Christ. The power that reigns in this world (aion and cosmos) by default is the influence of the fallen ruler. The world's default setting is strife, guilt, shame, rejection, and pain, necessitating our adoption by the Spirit. That's why the Bible says in Romans 8:15, "For you did not receive the spirit of slavery to fall back into fear, but you have received the Spirit of adoption as sons, by whom we cry, "Abba! Father!"

From early childhood, we wrestle with issues of possession and jealousy, but we must eventually realize that we cannot keep taking what belongs to others. Every toddler quickly realizes what they want, and strips those items from the hands of people screaming "mine!" But that carnal nature isn't really our portion for life. God has blessed us with a creative nature. We are made in his image, capable of creating and building beautiful things just like he did. No matter how vast and wild our creations might be, they are still within God's limitless domain.

God is the source of light that dispels the darkness—an inability to see and hear. He has dealt with guilt, shame, and rejection through the sacrifice of Christ on the cross, liberating us from the chains of judgment. He has also broken down the structures and patterns of the fallen world, freeing us from their limiting grip. Yet we often allow ourselves to operate within the boundaries defined by humanity and society. We need to question ourselves: Are we limiting our potential and our business's potential within a structure crafted by man? The world, as we know it, operates under a fallen ruler stripped of authority. Life may seem hard, filled with problems, until we start moving in the Spirit, embracing righteousness, peace, and joy. Satan, the fallen ruler, has no power and no authority. He can only deceive, but God has given us the power and authority to crush his head when he strikes our heels.

We must remember this when we create, launch, and solve problems through our businesses. The authority under which we operate is our choice. We can either live under the deceptive influence of a fallen angel, or we can embrace the divine authority bestowed upon us by God through faith in Christ. You were created to unlock the provisions of eternity, to rule over darkness, and bring supernatural solutions to worldly issues. Once you grasp the magnitude of your purpose, you'll realize it surpasses anything you could ever imagine.

This shift in perspective is a crucial transformation that must occur if one is to successfully bridge the gap to experiencing the infinite in both personal life and business on an everyday basis. Understanding this opens the eyes and ears of our spirits and souls. If you feel spiritually stagnant, it's not that you're incapable of hearing or that the Holy Spirit isn't communicating with you. It's more about being aware and receptive, about having your spiritual eyes and ears open, ready to perceive what is being revealed by the Spirit. If I tell my son to look for rocks that look like faces on the side of a cliff in nature, he will search until he finds them.

This Holy Spirit, your guide to Truth, will grant you access to the eternal wisdom that drives powerful and effective results, unaffected by the earthly forces at play in this cosmos, but if you want to see them, you have to seek until you find. We often forget to open our hearts and request His spiritual insights - to truly see and hear. In all honesty, many have never even been taught that there is a Holy Spirit, or that He seeks to communicate with us to provide dynamic instruction for life. As a result of a lack of awareness, many fail perpetually in humanistic cycles of what "we can do" only until our formulas and models fail because they are basic and regurgitated models of broken worldly systems.

Ask yourself this: Are you confident in your belief that you have the ability to see and hear what the Holy Spirit is wanting to reveal to you by revelation? Be honest with your answer; it's of utmost importance.

"Look at the birds of the air: they neither sow nor reap nor gather into barns, and yet your heavenly Father feeds them. Are you not of more value than they?" (Matthew 6:26 ESV)

This oft-quoted biblical passage about God's care for the birds leading to even greater care for us, isn't an invitation to see ourselves as helpless creatures begging for leftovers. Nor should we follow the avian example of perpetual sameness, building identical nests generation after generation with no sign of innovation. There are no grand bird-made structures, no avian skyscrapers. The reason is simple: You, unlike the birds, are meant to express creativity, to unleash the power of Intelligent Design. Without walking in the Spirit of God, you're likely operating at a mere 5% of your potential, whether you're a millionaire CEO or not. Unless you are seeking and applying heavenly strategies, you have hardly scratched the surface of your potential inheritance. If you're not moving in innovative ways, you're simply following what has already been done, just like the birds.

Sadly, this is a message the majority of the religious community fails to convey, often because they themselves do not walk in the Spirit. It's no one's fault per se, it's more about neglect: the Church has been neglecting the Spirit as much as the world does. This neglect leads to empty religious buildings, ineffective systems, and disgruntled individuals missing the real issue at hand: the importance of ruling in this world in every area of life with divine strategies. But don't lose hope. There exists a remnant of people on Earth who walk in the full power of God, including me and many of my associates. It is our mission to empower others to do the same. I am certain about the validity of this path and am ready to demonstrate it to you so that you can learn to walk this path too. If I can give you a present-day "follow me as I follow Christ", I aim to do it.

Realigning your perspective is crucial for effectively incorporating the eternal aspect into your life and business routine. It's about being aware and receptive to what the Father wants to speak to you right now by His Spirit. It's not about an inability to hear; it's about having the openness to hear and perceive what the Spirit communicates. The hard truth is this, you either will or you won't, and that's up to you.

Those who are aware and receptive can hear and see the Holy Spirit's guidance. The Spirit, in turn, provides access to eternal wisdom that fosters potent results, unhindered by the controlling forces of the cosmos. Yet, you may not have sought the awareness to perceive this. So, take note of this, reflect on it:

Do you truly believe and are you confident in your ability to perceive the Spirit's guidance?

Address this question with utmost honesty. It's essential to acknowledge this. We are not akin to birds relying on trees for sustenance. The Biblical analogy of God caring for birds and therefore caring even more for humans, is not a reflection of us being like birds living dependent on earthly means for life. Moreover, unlike birds that build the same nests generation after generation without innovation, humans have the innate ability to be creative and contribute to intelligent design. However, this capacity is mostly unutilized unless one walks in the Spirit of God. Remember, you're operating at merely about 5% capacity when not walking in the Spirit, regardless of your professional success.

Please, don't assess this book based on preconceived notions about the Church. Look beyond human failures in Jesus' name and focus on the works of God. Statistics show that a significant portion of the global Christian population doesn't even listen to the Holy Spirit despite the biblical assurance of His accessibility. 80% of the global Christian church claims to believe in Jesus, but not engage with the Holy Spirit. That's just sad, and quite honestly, stupid.

Throughout this book, let's set aside these trends and individually discern the relevance of this path. Does God desire to communicate with you? Does he wish to provide you with strategies for your business? I assure you that he does, but I urge you to seek confirmation from God himself. The Bible encourages us to strive towards God's presence, promising that His words would inspire obedience. It tells us in Hebrews 4 to boldly approach the throne of grace to find mercy and grace in times of need, including personal, professional, or relational needs. When you seek the Holy Spirit, you can transform your business into a source of joy, instead of simply a method of financial fortitude.

As part of this journey, I aim to connect the power of prophets with leaders, following the divine path laid by my Father. You may not have encountered this before, but remember, even those who didn't believe in God, like Pharaoh or King Nebuchadnezzar, were provided prophets from God who offered insights and warnings, instructions and strategies. The greatest kings of the earth have holy prophets at their side providing insight. Prophets have always been advisors to great leaders, helping them understand what they see and hear. Even if you doubt your ability to communicate with the Holy Spirit, you can benefit from the presence of someone who can.

Remain skeptical if you wish, but prophets are real. God's reputation can withstand your skepticism. Consider the story of a real prophet who challenged 850 false prophets (of baal and ashtoreth) to call down fire upon their altars on the top of a mountain. They called down fire but nothing happened. Despite drenching his altar in water, God's fire consumed the altar, leaving the false prophets with no choice but to acknowledge the one true God. So, stay skeptical if you wish, but remember, the choice to accept the truth about God is yours to decide. Although, I do have a question.

Are you willing to present your business at the mountaintop?
To lay it on the altar, inviting divine intervention?

It's a challenge, but it's worth considering, especially if you're willing to see whether or not divine fire doesn't show up in power to ignite your endeavors and confirm your true calling.

Remember, if God doesn't show up, it's not on you—it's on Him. But let me assure you, He has never failed to show up; He's promised to be there and has always fulfilled His promises.

As we step into this divine endeavor, let's strive to comprehend His will, along with the underutilized 95% capacity, and the strategies from heaven for our businesses through the power of pure communication with the Holy Spirit. This is an invitation to transcend from our 'worldly' plane and connect with the power of our Creator to expand the works we put our hands to by obeying His ways instead of our own.

So, let's venture into this journey with our businesses, extending them beyond the mundane to meet the spiritual power available to us at the mountaintop. And let's observe the transformation that follows. God is waiting to embrace us at the summit, to set ablaze our endeavors with His divine flame. We may not know what lies ahead, but we can rest assured that God will be there. The future of your business can't be predicted precisely on our own, but the Father's presence and instruction by the Holy Spirit can be counted upon. It's time to venture forward with the courage and determination needed to unlock the heavenly strategy meant for you.

If you've never followed the Holy Spirit in your business, this transformation might seem like a daunting change, but it's not! It's an adventure of identity, and you will see massive growth even on a personal level. No matter how high you might raise your eyebrow, God isn't offended. Instead, He's excited to show you His glory. He is willing and capable of proving His might to you.

Are you ready to take this leap? Are you willing to place your faith in the Father, to tap into the potential He's embedded in your DNA, and to discover what your business can truly become? If so, let's start this journey together, meet God on the mountaintop, and watch as He brings down the fire to invigorate our businesses in the presence of our enemies like never before.

For those of you who may be reading this and have not yet put your faith in Christ, I want you to consider something. I might even make other believers mad for saying this, but it's still true. You don't need to be a believer in Jesus to glean wisdom from the teachings of his prophets. As we continue this conversation, we're going to delve deeper into the power of Truth, probably in ways you've never heard before. If I am positioned to be the anointed voice that relays strategies from the Father, then so be it. Just as Joseph and Daniel spoke to unbelieving kings, I'm willing to reveal strategies that will leave you no choice but to say "HE IS THE ONE TRUE GOD!"

If you're unsure about Jesus, unsure about making a commitment to listen to the voice of the Holy Spirit, that's fine for now. Just keep reading. While I would encourage you to make that leap, it's your decision. All I'm doing is sharing what I know to be true, what I know is available to you. As you learn, I believe you'll see why this relationship with God is my everything. Proverbs

25:2 tells us "it's the glory of God to conceal matters, and it's the glory of kings to seek them out". Are you ready, as a king or queen, to uncover the hidden treasures stored for you in heaven? If so, it's time to 'honor a prophet,' not just for a one-sided reward, but for mutual empowerment. I'm speaking in principle here. I'm actually not a prophet. Technically, I'm an apostle in the Kingdom, but track with me here and you'll see why I brought this up.

In the company of a prophet, you'll reap the benefits of their identity, but the benefits are activated through honor, not just through presence. Even when Pharaoh and Nebuchadnezzar benefited from the insights of holy prophets, it was because they honored what God was doing through Joseph and Daniel. This is about trust, remember? As we've discussed, the power of pure communication nurtures trust. Trust, in turn, holds our inheritance. To access that inheritance, we must go to those trusts and draw from them. Often, we draw our inheritance from the trusts we have in the people he sends our way.

Banks have obligations. Just as they hold our deposits for us to withdraw, so too do our relationships demand deposits and withdrawals to establish trust. The trust fund that's cultivated in relationships will release your inheritance, providing the necessary resources to fuel your legacy, but you have to actually steward those relationships. I want you to write this down: "Deposits and withdrawals in your relationships develop trust. This trust fund releases your inheritance to fuel your legacy." Keep this thought close, especially when considering your professional relationships, your team, your hires, and your employers.

Let's take this to our businesses. The more you honor your colleagues, the more their identities are released. The rewards of honor in the right relationships can bestow a mantle of grace that positions you to move in eternal authority in your life. Yes, that's spiritual, but it doesn't make it any less real. The spiritual realm is more real and lasting than the physical realm, I guarantee that. Think about it from this perspective: as a business owner, entrepreneur, or leader, have you ever contemplated the idea of divine anointment for your role? Have you ever considered that you have been anointed and positioned with great purpose to fulfill a mission that has eternal significance? If this concept is new to you, let's explore the notion of the anointing. Honor, in all its forms, has a reciprocal effect. Honor a prophet as a prophet, you receive a prophet's reward. Honor a righteous person as such, and receive a righteous person's reward. This pattern holds across all relationships. Honor a teacher as a teacher, and you will receive a teacher's reward. With all that being said, what do people receive when they honor you? What is it that you carry in the spiritual realm for people to take hold of when they honor you?

Extend this principle to your business. By honoring those involved, their identities are liberated, their God-given creativity is unleashed to benefit your business and the people in it. Let's say you hire a copywriter. If you work closely with them, as they honor your desires, you will impart a portion of your identity and purpose into their work, allowing them to produce better results more tailored to the specific need or expression. This is the power of honor. Communication happens at a personal level, both parties benefit greatly, and both are rewarded with an activation for greater works. As you honor your team, they will want to be in your presence, where the purest communication is fostered.

Don't be surprised when you find yourself enjoying the process of understanding people better. Lean into that and it will ignite a deep ability for knowing how to lead them, merely by spending time with them. That's the work of the Holy Spirit within you, teaching you the power of accessing new realms of increase through your willingness to see, hear, and honor the people around you. Yes, you are important and want people to receive from your presence, but you should also realize that every relationship you steward in honor will impart something new to you, empowering you to go further, faster, because you accessed the power of pure communication.

I urge you to think of yourself as a shepherd in your business. There is a current divine movement happening on earth, and it is a shepherding movement. It's time for leaders like you to embrace what I call "the power of pastoral reformation in business". By learning to truly listen and understand those around you, even beyond the scope of professional matters, you will lead more effectively. Honoring the purpose in people's lives, in essence, releases an impartation between both parties. Remember: Honoring a prophet yields a prophet's reward. Honoring a righteous person yields a righteous person's reward. If you honor a copywriter as a copywriter, you might just find yourself reaping a copywriter's reward. But just how far can this lead, and why is it important? It sounds simple...because it is. But what can this really produce in your life, and how far can you really take the power of honoring people?

Communication lies at the heart of human interaction. But, in the realm of business, or in any other field for that matter, the manner of our communication can be turned into provision for increase, abundance, and opportunity. For the unbelievers reading this book, the common principles and teachings that prevail from your efforts to pay attention to the voices and anointings of others may not necessarily resonate with your own current values and beliefs. But just because it's different, it doesn't make it wrong. Take a moment to reflect on this thought: Pure communication, fueled by the Holy Spirit's instructions, will result in impartations that dynamically reveal and confirm the anointing upon your life for the things that God has led you to build. Simultaneously, this will also confirm the identities of those you lead, providing incredible opportunity to lead and position those people for greatness. This isn't a mere simple concept, but a profound truth, so fiery that it bears repeating.

You mustn't block everyone out after conversing with the Holy Spirit. The same open-hearted discourse you have with the Spirit should mirror the way you converse with the people in your life. It's not enough to simply ask for guidance and walk away, expecting instant solutions. Sometimes, the answers from the Holy Spirit require your silence. Silence to listen, patience to understand, and persistence to ensure you hear His voice. But silence is meant for listening, not for leading. Once you know what to do, you have to share those plans with your people.

When you do, you should also listen to their responses, and observe what they do with the instructions. What will Holy Spirit inspired instructions do to the dynamics of your business and the community you're leading amongst the people who steward assignments in your endeavors?

These principles of communication, powered by the Holy Spirit, need to be the basis of all your relationships, especially in your business. This strategy can manifest in various forms. At times, it can take the form of spiritual insights. Other times, it can manifest as supernatural wisdom in business, such as a copywriter churning out the best copy you've ever read, or you obtaining a solution to a problem you didn't even know existed.

A personal anecdote is worth sharing here. Once, while working for a company in the oil and gas industry, I was invited to a strategy meeting to discuss ideas for developing greater impact of protocols throughout the business at a "field work" level. The real issue was that the corporate office had been dishing out all kinds of new rules and regulations, aimed to create a more solid infrastructure for operations at the field level. I was the only field operative amidst executives. As they discussed safety protocols, new rules, and their desire to see fruit from these implementations, the Holy Spirit provided me with a strategy to release to the executives in that room that astounded even the highly-paid consultants in the room. In fact, I was emailed just after the meeting with an offer to take a corporate position and transfer to the corporate office 5 hours away. This was not because I was smarter than anyone else, but because I sought guidance from an unseen presence in the room. (Yes... the Holy Spirit.) I was able to redirect perspectives onto the real issue, solving problems they didn't realize existed, while their minds were headed in an entirely different direction.

Many businesses exist out of sync with their Creator's plans. They feel more like jobs than opportunities for creative expressions through the owners' and employees' identity and creativity. This misalignment is often due to business strategies that were created by others, not birthed through individuals. This dissonance creates frustration and can be remedied by aligning business operations with the people's true identities and creative expressions. This alignment not only establishes a pastoral reformation within business but also allows for the unlocking of true identities and strategies. These revelations, in turn, fuel the growth of your business. As you begin to integrate the Holy Spirit into your communication, others in your presence will also catch the fire and the strategies. How? Because you will be setting a new standard for operations, while inviting the Creator of all things to the table.

For instance, in my own business, we have leaders who communicate and check on others consistently, sharing Holy Spirit strategies and facilitating life changes. Our alignment with the Holy Spirit has resulted in supernatural growth and interesting strategies. Our obedience is pretty radical, such as running an ad campaign from a vision that reads, "your socks stink." That ad actually created positive ROI, even when it sounded ridiculous at the time. This approach to leadership and communication might be at odds with traditional models. Yet, not every organization claiming to be Christian even follows these principles. More attention needs to be paid to the concepts of shepherding, obedience to the Holy Spirit, and a willingness to do things differently. Leaders must be present, invested in their people, and guided by the Holy Spirit.

Let me talk to the intrapreneurs and employees for a moment.

If your current leaders or advisors aren't showing this level of commitment and interest, it may be time to reassess those relationships. An effective leader is one who invests not just their time and resources, but also their heart into their people. Leadership isn't about governing from a high tower; it's about walking side-by-side with those you lead, understanding their trials, and championing their successes. Just as it is in personal relationships, the leadership bond in business or any organization requires a two-way street of communication. If you're not being heard or your needs aren't being addressed, the partnership may no longer serve your growth.

Consider the following:

Are your leaders providing you with the time and attention you require to flourish in your assignment?

Are they contributing constructively to your development?

Are they taking the time to understand your needs, your dreams, your fears?

Are they helping you walk the path of your divine purpose?

If the answers are not affirmative, it might be an indication that it's time for change. This change doesn't necessarily have to be abrupt. It could start with a conversation expressing your concerns and needs. If there's no positive outcome from this dialogue, then you might want to explore new options. Sometimes you can be the catalyst for change even when you're not the leader, but if the spark doesn't ignite the flame, you might need to move.

If you're an internal worker who comes alongside leaders to help them build, surround yourself with leaders who embody the principles of a Spirit-led shepherd. They should be individuals who listen and offer guidance, who lead with a spirit of service and genuine interest in your well-being, and who are willing to follow the insights and instruction from the Holy Spirit, even when they come from people at the "bottom of the totem pole". In essence, seek out those who embody a Holy Spirit-driven approach in their leadership style. Align yourself with leaders who lead through the Spirit, nurturing a culture of honesty, authenticity, and compassion. This alignment will not only nourish your personal and professional growth but will also catalyze a shift in your business dynamics, resulting in success and fulfillment beyond measure.

The Holy Spirit's guidance and instructions are invaluable resources in our life journey. By integrating His teachings into our communication strategies, we foster relationships that reflect His love, foster unity, and drive purpose-driven growth. Whether in sales or leadership, the infusion of the Holy Spirit into our communication can initiate a transformation that transcends our mere human understanding. Embrace this transformative power and the beauty of Holy Spirit-inspired communication in every aspect of your life. Allow it to redefine your relationships, reorient your business, and reshape your world. This is the path to unlocking not only your own true identity but also the divine potential that lies within every connection you make. This is the power of pure communication.

If you want to make more money, build more people. This philosophy resonates strongly when the building is done with Holy Spirit-led communication. It's not about just business transactions; it's about fostering relationships, revealing identities, unlocking strategies, and birthing a future aligned with God's divine blueprint.

At this point, I would like you to reflect on your journey. Take a moment and assess the leadership dynamics surrounding you. Do you have leaders, coaches, mentors, and advisors who genuinely take an interest in you and your journey and provide instruction, insights, and guidance driven by the Holy Spirit? Or do you feel like you're stuck with templates and strategies that feel secondhand, not tailored to your unique needs and circumstances?

I urge you not to settle for leadership that doesn't provide individual attention and intention. If the people guiding you don't make time for you or aren't actively interested in your journey, it might be time to let them go. In my own journey, if I've hired a coach or an advisor who fails to pay attention to my needs, providing me with nothing more than empty systems, I don't hesitate to terminate that relationship. Because you see, I refuse to build my business on secondhand strategies. Imagine walking in someone else's old, worn shoes; the fit is uncomfortable and the path uncertain. You wouldn't want that for your personal life, and I'm sure you wouldn't want it for your business either, would you?

Let's not fool ourselves into thinking these impersonal, cookie-cutter strategies will get us anywhere. Instead, choose to be 'Fathered'. The Holy Spirit told me to deliver this message: "Don't be fooled. Be Fathered." Not by people, but by the Father in heaven. Be willing to have people in your life who mirror the Father more than the fool. Expect more from your leaders; they should reflect wisdom and divine guidance rather than foolish, ineffectual leadership. It's quite surprising how such a simple act can yield powerful results.

To advance this further, let me teach you how to activate communications. The key to communication is "questions." Questions, as we all know, pave the way for answers. That sounds obvious, right? But how often do we harness the power of asking questions in our businesses? When was the last time you asked the right question that led to a solution you desperately needed? Don't let pride or fear of appearing vulnerable deter you from asking questions. There's no harm in admitting when you're struggling or worried. You don't have to bottle it up for fear of scaring your team. Instead, lean on them, ask them questions, and seek their counsel. You might be surprised at the wisdom they possess, and the way they respond to being honored. It doesn't matter if you're the top leader at the company or the lowest paid member of your team. Ask questions that demand mighty responses.

Similarly, consider the problems and questions your people may have. Sometimes, just being present can encourage them to ask you for guidance. That's when you can deliver the answers they seek, guided by the Holy Spirit. "Ask and tell" – it's a simple principle that can revolutionize your leadership.

Reflecting on my own journey, I started my business at the age of 26. The first year and a half to two years were spent building out our school. But it wasn't until May 2020 that we launched the school in its fullness. In the time span of just over a year, we grew from being a one-person operation to a team of over 20, and I was already nearing my first million in revenue before I was 30. This growth was not just in terms of numbers. The true measure of our success was the profound impact we had on people's lives. The heartfelt thank-you notes, the gratitude for our dedication, the life-altering changes people experienced – these were our real victories. Marriages were saved, families were healed, and a positive ripple effect was created in every aspect of life.

In the following chapters, we'll explore more about the power of people in business. But before that, here's some homework for you:

1. How confident are you, right now, that you have access to the Holy Spirit's instructions, even if you haven't learned to listen for them yet?

2. Does the thought of seeking guidance from the Holy Spirit for your business bring you peace or anxiety?

3. Do you feel a newfound hope or are you feeling confused, perhaps even left out, as if you truly don't have access?

Reflect on why you feel the way you do about these questions. These are not simply rhetorical questions but exercises meant to spark deep introspection. Once you have your answers, I encourage you to share them with someone, perhaps even to a larger audience through a live video in a group. The act of voicing your thoughts can bring further clarity and will open up space for collective engagement and growth. Moreover, this exercise could be the first step towards breaking down any barriers that may have been preventing you from fully accessing and harnessing divine guidance in your business. So, go on, take this small step. Reflect, question, share, and, most importantly, listen to what the Holy Spirit may be trying to tell you. Remember, your leadership journey isn't a path you need to tread alone. You have access to the most extraordinary guidance, and all it requires is your faith, your willingness to listen, and the courage to act on what you hear. It's time to let go of secondhand strategies and embrace a leadership approach that's uniquely yours, guided by the wisdom of the Holy Spirit.

As we move forward in the subsequent chapters of this book, we'll dive deeper into this concept, exploring how you can leverage the power of people and the conversation you hold with the Holy Spirit to take your leadership—and your business—to new heights. Stay tuned, as I'll cover practical steps, share even more powerful insights, and provide further exercises to help you build the strong, effective, and Spirit-led leadership style that your business needs.

CHAPTER 2: THE ART
OF IMPRESSION

In this chapter, we are going to unlock the secrets of "The Art of Impression." This art will serve as your next step in creating a business that truly rejoices, illuminating your path to the Creator's design by utilizing the most precious resources you have - the people within your business. I will also introduce you to new concepts that will further enhance your understanding and application of this art. So, buckle up and get ready to venture on this journey of discovery and enlightenment. Welcome to chapter two of teaching your business to rejoice!

To explain the Art of Impression, let me share a story about someone from my own business. His name is Justin, an amazing man and the dean of The King's Company. I witnessed firsthand his incredible power and resilience during a challenging time at the beach. We were there to pray for someone who was wrestling with a great deal of negativity and, quite frankly, I'd had enough. It was time for us to invoke the power of God.

An unfortunate situation arose when a client at our school was battling with COVID. The virus was taking a severe toll on her; she struggled with even the simplest tasks, like getting dressed. On the day we visited her, she could barely breathe. Despite the expectation for everyone to wear masks and sanitize, I was resolute in my faith. I removed her mask, declared her body as holy ground, and commanded the virus to leave her body. Miraculously, COVID immediately receded, leaving her completely healed.

It was on this day that I realized there was immense power in shepherding within my business. The opportunity to directly influence and impact people's lives is both rewarding and humbling. I desired to do more of this, to touch more lives in such a profound way.

Later that night, while at the beach with my family, I noticed that Justin was conducting a live session on Facebook. He was fully engaged, hosting what we call Kingdom Life Discussions. Over three hours into his session, I was amazed to discover that he was praying for people to be healed - and they were. In that moment, I realized that there was an extension of me, working tirelessly to bring about healing and transformation. Justin was operating in his full identity, making a difference in people's lives within a business that was created through my obedience. This was a profound realization for me. The Art of Impression isn't just about making an impact; it's about enabling others to operate in their true identities. Leaders need to create space for their teams to be true to themselves, because when they do, it triggers a significant shift - it changes something.

Here's the crux of the matter: anything caused by sin is cured by love. Negative, dark, and unhealthy elements of the world that cause disease, weakness, and sickness can all be healed by love. The Bible itself tells us that love covers a multitude of sins. This means if love can make an appearance it can heal the sick, it can heal the pain, and it can heal any problems we face.

The Lord has reminded me that in our current generation, a pastoral reformation is being released in the world. This reformation is manifested through what I call Shepherding Movements. These movements are imbued with principles of shepherding that will release power in your business. I've experienced it in my own business. When I showed up and was fully present for someone, I was able to connect with the Holy Spirit and declare healing over their body, resulting in immediate recovery. What was this phenomenon? I believe that when the love of God, moving through obedience to the leading of the Holy Spirit, is released through the voice of a shepherd, it produces a unique frequency or sound that can vanquish disease and sickness.

Reflecting on John 8, it is noted that Jesus went through a region where he taught in the synagogue, healed every single sick person, cast out all the demons, and preached the gospel of the kingdom. His actions here were not random; they were part of his shepherding mission. As he was leaving the region, he saw that the people were like sheep without a shepherd: weak and helpless. He told his disciples to pray that the Lord of the harvest would send more workers into his fields. This verse serves as a vivid reminder of the power of shepherding, a power that Jesus himself embodied and demonstrated.

Shepherding, in its truest form, involves teaching, healing, and nurturing - leading your flock not just towards earthly prosperity, but spiritual enrichment as well. The power of shepherding is transformative; it affects all aspects of life and business, enabling growth, prosperity, and healing. In my experience, the power of shepherding can release a divine frequency that carries the ability to heal diseases and overcome adversities. The love of God, made known by the voice of a true shepherd, through the power of the Holy Spirit, releases a sound that has the power to cure sickness, doubts, emotional distress, inadequacy... anything really.

I believe, quite strongly, that our generation is poised for a pastoral reformation, a new era where Shepherding Movements will take center stage. These movements, rooted in the principles of shepherding, will serve as catalysts for change, ushering in a wave of healing, transformation, and empowerment within our businesses.

Remember, God has a rich harvest ready for us. He is eager to bless us abundantly through our businesses. The key to accessing this divine harvest lies in understanding and practicing the Art of Impression, and in harnessing the transformative power of shepherding. As we strive to be true shepherds, creating space for our team to operate in their true identities, we will unlock the door to infinite blessings and breakthroughs in our businesses. Let's embark on this journey of shepherding transformation together, shaping the future of our businesses, and the world, one step at a time.

Some individuals hold the belief that the only platform for reaching people and spreading the Word of God is through the local church. However, I am a testament to the fact that one can reach people in various ways, including through business. There is a vast, untapped opportunity in business to affect significant change and to be a part of the harvest. By understanding and harnessing the power of shepherding, we can reach and influence countless individuals.

The power that comes with shepherding is transformative. When the love of God is released through the Holy Spirit and the voice of a committed shepherd, lives are profoundly changed. This change is born of the fundamental belief that anything caused by sin can be cured by love. As such, to establish a potent and influential business that moves in great power through people, one must strive to create a shepherding movement. This movement ensures that the people involved in your business shine, and in so doing, your business thrives. As this transformation takes place, individuals, families, and lives are healed because love has the power to cure sin and cover a multitude of sins. What if your business could provide amazing products, services, and financial increase, while also releasing the power that heals, sets free, and points people to the One True God?

Reflecting on yet another incident involving Justin, I'm reminded of the concept of 'impression.' When I shared a post on Facebook praising Justin as a Godly man whose actions impress me, I was moved to consider the term 'impress' in a different light. It dawned on me that the word 'impress' can carry two definitions. It's not just about being awestruck by someone, though that's part of it. But in the context I'm referring to, 'impress' means to make a mark or design on an object using a stamp or seal. In this context, Justin, through his shepherding and obedience to the divine will, left a mark on me - an impression of the Divine Designer working through him. This impression added to my identity, enriching it. The same will happen when your team members, in their shepherd's obedience and love for those they lead, leave a mark on you. You will find your identity enhanced and transformed.

Jesus, in one of His teachings, said, "I will make you fishers of men," emphasizing the divine intent to make us influential. The phrase underscores the divine will and desire to shape us into influential beings. This process happens through divine design, as we willingly receive the divine code that releases eternal identity through our words, actions, creations, and deeds. See, the most important word in that verse is "make." I will 'make' you fishers of men. This means that He is not done creating us, not done making us, not finished designing us, and this ongoing creation is our portion!

Understanding the true power of unity is essential in this context. Unity is not about arguing to establish common ground. Rather, it is about honoring each individual in your community or business, allowing them to be who they were created to be. It is about making room for their voice, their ideas, and their perspectives. As they express their divine design, they will leave a mark on you, transforming your perception and understanding of their anointing while simultaneously continuing the creative design of your own identity in a process of perpetual edification. It will also create a platform that prioritizes people over systems and models.

Consider this: God, the best Creator, built the Church on the foundation of people - apostles, prophets, and the Messiah (Christ as the Cornerstone). If we desire to build our businesses like the best Creator, we need to build it on people and not systems or models. We need to create a space where people can freely express their divine identity, where the divine designer can work through them to raise the level of the business and benefit everyone involved.

To fully understand the power of unity, it's also essential to honor people not only for the divine inspiration expressed through them but also for the skills they have developed and honed. The parable of the talents illustrates this. A master gives his servants money to invest or grow, each according to their own abilities. The servant who hides his talent, out of fear, is not making full use of his skills. Either way, the funds were distributed by the Master according to the abilities that each one had already developed in their lives.

In the Parable of the Talents, a master leaves his servants with various amounts of money, or "talents", to manage during his absence. The servants who invest their talents, growing them from two to four or from five to ten, are praised for their good stewardship. Meanwhile, the servant who buried his talent in the ground, making no profit at all, is rebuked by the master. This is an example of stewardship based on the individual's abilities and serves as an important principle we can apply to our business operations. Those who honor their gifts, identity, and who develop abilities are worthy of delegation in greater measure.

If you wish to create an impression and make a substantial impact on your business, you need to recognize and utilize the abilities of the people in your organization. Ask yourself, "Do I really understand what the people in my business are capable of?" Their capabilities should inform how you delegate responsibilities. By consulting with the Holy Spirit, asking for guidance on the suitability of each person for their role, you can structure your business based on people rather than systems.

A successful business is like a well-tended flock. As a good shepherd, you must lead your sheep to pastures that nourish them, that give them the right nutrients for the journey ahead. The same applies to your team; placing them in roles (or even creating new roles and responsibilities) that allow them to flourish, ensuring the healthy growth of your business. This practice I'll refer to as the "art of shepherding," and it fosters not only business efficiency but also a culture of love, honor, and transformational relationships.

This brings us to the concept of transactional versus transformational relationships. The former are purely about exchanges - you provide a service or product, and you receive payment in return. The latter, however, are deeper. They foster mutual growth, synergy, and a sense of community, belonging, and personal purpose in the mandate being fulfilled. By recognizing and cultivating transformational relationships within your organization, you can tap into their inherent potential and convert transactional ones into transformational ones, leading to significant and intentional change and growth.

It's important to remember that people are the solution carriers in your business. The greater your understanding of their individual identities, the more successful your business can be. So ask yourself, "Do I understand the difference between transactional relationships in my business versus transformational relationships in my business?" If you discover that some relationships are purely transactional, consider this a chance to tap into untapped potential for your business.

Beyond understanding your employees' identities, hearing from God and receiving heavenly revelations about them will also aid in fostering transformational relationships. Some business leaders may simply want their employees to follow a strict model, to obey and perform specific tasks. However, this approach lacks power and depth. Instead, strive to learn the hearts of your people.

In a vision, I once saw myself leading an army into battle. In the midst of the fight, the hand of the Lord came down and grabbed my shirt. God held me back, not to restrict me but to make me observe. God wanted me to understand the hearts of my warriors, to comprehend their willingness to fight for me. I wanted to lead from the front, but He wanted me to observe from behind as people rushed into battle before me. This revelation led to a transition in my leadership style. We created opportunities and positions that would allow each individual to be the full expression of who they already are, rather than forcing them to fall in line, into a predetermined mold.

This approach allows for rapid growth and a system where I can learn who people truly are, identify their skills and abilities, and integrate them into the perfect role in our business. It's about empowering individuals rather than holding them back in the wrong roles and positions, allowing them to fulfill their potential and contribute to the success of the business the way they were designed to. By embodying the spirit of a good shepherd, you can foster a culture of honor and understanding, transforming your business into a thriving, dynamic organism.

In the realm of business, it's essential to comprehend the

difference between leading and losing. To have a thriving enterprise, you should aim to be at the forefront of delegating based on identity, leading your people into greater expressions of their dynamic nature, rather than being at the losing end of a battle, placing people in roles that you feel need to be present based on a traditional model that seemingly worked in the past. One significant strategy to accomplish this is to create an environment where every voice in your company is acknowledged and valued. You may instinctively disregard certain individuals who may appear less significant in the conventional business realm, yet these individuals often harbor untapped potential. Recognizing this potential can yield unprecedented success and fulfillment. However, even when this concept makes sense, the revelation for leading people can still seem out of reach from moment to moment. That's why we need to also consider the power of prophetic roundtables.

Drawing inspiration from historical practices, it's noteworthy to consider how ancient kings didn't just rely on one-on-one consultations with prophets to receive instruction from heaven. Rather, they sought the collective wisdom of councils of prophets —forming what we'll refer to as 'prophetic roundtables'. This may seem like an antiquated or peculiar approach in the context of modern business, but upon application, it has been found to offer significant benefits. As an example, a group of individuals known for their prophetic insights were engaged to deliberate on my own company's vision. This unique assembly didn't just provide intriguing perspectives but also birthed invaluable strategies for business growth—both financially and in terms of community development.

Reflecting on biblical narratives, particularly from Acts chapter two, there's a remarkable instance where the Holy Spirit was poured out on a group gathered in an upper room. Don't you want the same to happen in your business meetings? Applying this spiritual reality and opportunity to business, consider the transformative potential if a similar divine outpouring could occur within your company. The concept of a 'prophetic roundtable' emerges here as a practical application, where leaders, team members, and prophetic voices meet. While some might initially find this strange, it's a gathering that could catalyze solutions, strategies, and new pathways to success.

Continuing this ideal, consider this: Every successful business enterprise hinges on the identification and application of solutions. One effective way to foster a solution-oriented culture is through the creation of 'solutionary roundtables'. These are spaces devoted to addressing specific issues or topics. What type of "room" or "roundtable" could you create within your business to create space for the Holy Spirit to speak into your business through your people? A "war room" full of those who have been identified as solutionaries could serve as a hub for tackling complex problems, embracing a collective gathering in a strategy room for crafting marketing or sales plans, a visionary room for conceptualizing future strategies, or an innovation conversation room for brainstorming novel ideas.

Instituting these solutionary rooms and implementing the strategies discussed within them can cause a fundamental shift in your business. The Book of Daniel in the Bible provides an intriguing parallel here. As Daniel received revelation and strategy through prophetic insights, modern businesses might similarly benefit from this approach. My suggestion is that this transition towards incorporating more prophetic insights into business strategy might be part of what's referred to as the 'pastoral reformation'. This is a movement anticipated to sweep across all industries and cultures. This offers businesses a unique opportunity to not only be part of this transition but to shape and influence the direction of their industries. What if your business became the revolutionary catalyst to industry change, simply because you were willing to pay attention to both the Holy Spirit, and the people within your business?

In the world of business, an opportunity awaits you to model innovative, pioneering strategies that revolve around people. Rest assured, this approach will serve as a learning platform for fostering better interpersonal relationships. We're not used to this type of leadership, because we are culturally systematized to follow a more democratic and governmental leadership style and pattern. We should understand that placing faith in "government" to rectify issues may not always lead to the desired outcomes. Rather, believing in and investing in people tends to yield more productive results. This is what Jesus taught. Even though he implemented a government of leaders in the church (the Five-fold ministries of the apostle, prophet, evangelist, pastor, and teacher), he taught and proved a greater principle - the least is the greatest in the Kingdom of heaven.

Consider this as well, while we're mentioning the government. A community of dedicated, purpose-driven individuals can effectively influence and transform governmental systems faster than relying solely on government entities to bring about societal changes. We can cultivate a new generation, even from those not yet born, to become influential leaders capable of reshaping the fabrics of society and culture in our spheres of influence and nations. It's a more plausible approach than attempting to persuade established governmental systems to initiate change. Just change things from the inside out by raising people into position through honoring their creative design in Christ.

The path forward is clear. We need to focus on developing our people, and the blessing of honoring people in business will manifest greater results more quickly than traditional methods. This doesn't necessitate obsessive monitoring of the activities to justify the process, but simply demands obedience to the Holy Spirit's guidance, allowing people to move at His pace, and stewarding the role of a shepherd as we watch him transform lives and industries through that obedience in our lives.

We should come together as Spirit-led leaders, not only within the confines of a physical church building, but in spaces created where we can address our business needs. These gatherings may occur in the various solutionary rooms we create: the war room, the visionary room, or any other specialized "room". As we build our businesses, we are concurrently assembling a congregation of individuals who are empowered by the divine power of the universe's Creator, our Father in heaven. We are given dominion to steward dynamic spaces as we lead uniquely created individuals.

Hosting this type of culture and community, and utilizing the creation of these rooms can become the defining aspects of our businesses. Populate them with dedicated individuals who excel in their respective domains. If your business needs a marketing strategy, for instance, create a solutionary room focused on that specific area, inviting the relevant experts. Add a few prophetic business consultants to the mix and engage in an enlightening exchange of ideas. Prophets bring a unique element to these gatherings, often creating an enjoyable, productive atmosphere without requiring pre-established agendas. They operate on divine insight. You have the ability to implement this within your own business by creating these solutionary rooms, and allowing the Holy Spirit to shape your business through your team.

When you foster a pastoral movement among your workforce and expose them to the power of God in your business realm, your business transcends the mere reflection of your individual identity. When you honor people, and let them reflect God's ideas and nature into your business, your business takes on a greater identity that what you personally envisioned in the beginning by yourself. Now, it reflects the total compromised nature of your empowered community, including the expressions of everyone honored. Reflect on this for a moment. Does the idea of your business embodying more than just your personal identity cause anxiety, or peace? If the business starts reflecting the identities of your team members, are you still comfortable with following the Holy Spirit's guidance?

The entrepreneurial journey, especially for those who have built their ventures from scratch, often leaves a strong imprint of their identity on their businesses. However, as the team grows and a communal creative force emerges, the collective identity begins to shape the business. If the notion of shared identity causes discomfort, it might reflect a tinge of selfishness, which can impede the expression of love and consequently hamper business growth.

Love is the antidote to the maladies caused by sin and self-centeredness. It keeps no record of wrong, doesn't envy, doesn't boast, and is not self-seeking. Infusing love into your business by establishing an internal shepherded movement can catalyze profound transformation. Our businesses provide solutions to heal people's pains, make life more enjoyable, or even solve the world's toughest problems. We need more businesses to solve bigger problems through the power of people, especially people who are guided by the Spirit of Truth. By approaching this necessity with love, you introduce a divine power into the industry that shifts the dynamics of opportunity while also shifting the influence upon people from transactional to transformational relationships.

In having a transformational relationship with an industry, thought leaders or innovators become synonymous with the field they operate in. Their transformative influence shines brightly, casting a far-reaching, impactful ripple across the industry. This is the power of a transformational relationship forged in love. With every breath, each word, and every collaboration, we strive to mold an environment rich with trust and faith, for that is the bedrock of our business. Yet, in the whirl of ambitions, pressures, and daily challenges, it's easy to lose sight of this grounding reality. But let's hit pause. Take a step back. Reflect on the principle that has guided us all along.

The Art of Impressions isn't just about making a mark, it's about leaving a legacy, an imprint of faith, integrity, and collaboration that not only shapes your business but also shapes lives. Imagine a Kingdom-minded business where everyone has a voice, where every contribution matters, where each idea is valued. That's the kind of business we're building. And if we're to ensure that this ethos permeates every aspect of our operations, we must make conscious efforts to nurture a culture of trust and empowerment. That's the only way we can genuinely say that our business is defined not just by the solutions we offer, but by the people we empower.

In the grand tapestry of this business, every person plays a role in weaving a pattern, adding a unique hue to the fabric. And the beauty of this intricate pattern lies not in its perfection, but in its authenticity. As shepherds of this grand design, we need to allow our people the freedom to contribute their uniqueness, to add their distinctive thread to the fabric. In the long run, it's this diversity of thought and perspective that will add depth and richness to our shared creation.

In our business, it's not just about the final product; it's about the process of creation. It's about the journey we undertake together, supporting and empowering one another along the way. It's about creating a space where everyone feels they belong, where they are valued and nurtured. And it's about cultivating a culture of unity and collaboration, where every success is shared, and every challenge is faced together. When that happens, the products and services we provide will abound in ingenuity, creativity, and power. This unity and togetherness, this sense of shared purpose and collective ownership, that's what sets us apart. This is what will sustain us as we continue to grow, as we continue to strive for greater heights. Because at the end of the day, the real strength of our business isn't in our products or services, it's in our people.

But business can still be 'busy' even when it's built on people rather than systems. We should never forget the importance of rest, reflection, and rejuvenation. They are vital to sustain our momentum and maintain our energy. Remember, we cannot pour from an empty cup. We must allow ourselves and our people the time to rejuvenate, to re-energize, and to refocus. As shepherds, it's our responsibility to create a balance that ensures not only our growth but also our well-being.

Finally, let us never forget the essence of the faith that underpins our journey. The principles we adhere to, the values we hold dear, and the faith that guides us, are all fundamental to our business. They are what bind us together, they give us the strength to face the odds, and they give us the confidence to chase our dreams.

We are all shepherds commissioned to lead in our metrons,

leading to the establishment of this grand design, empowered by the blood of Jesus to shape a business that's not just successful but also compassionate, collaborative, and faithful. Let us remember, we're not just building a business; we're building a legacy. One that's defined by the love, unity, and faith we've infused into it. So let's continue to create, innovate, and inspire. Let's continue to make room for every voice and idea. Let's continue to empower and uplift each other. Let's continue to be shepherds of faith and creators of lasting impressions. Together, we can make a difference, create a legacy, and shape a business that truly reflects the values we hold dear. A business that is a testament to our shared faith, a beacon of hope and a shining example of the power of unity and collaboration.

This shared vision and collective effort isn't just about business growth; it's about personal growth. It's about fostering an environment where individuals can thrive, reach their full potential, and, in doing so, contribute to collective success. That's how we build a legacy — by empowering our people, encouraging their unique talents, and providing them with the opportunity to flourish. Our legacy is not measured by the number of products we sell or the revenue we generate. Instead, it's gauged by the growth of our people, their successes, and their evolution. It's seen in the difference we make in people's lives, the values we impart, and the principles we instill. A business built on such a foundation of faith, compassion, and integrity to obey the Holy Spirit is truly a Kingdom Business. A business where everyone feels valued, where every voice is heard, and where everyone is given the chance to contribute, create, and grow. This is our legacy.

But a true Kingdom business needs not just builders, but also protectors, custodians who can safeguard the values, principles, and practices that form its very essence. As shepherds, this is our responsibility. Not only to lead and guide but also to protect and preserve. To ensure that the business we're building remains true to its core, to the faith that guides us, and to the people who make it what it is.

We must remember that our journey doesn't end with building

a successful business; it continues as we strive to sustain it, to evolve it, and to ensure that it stays true to its purpose. That's the real challenge, and that's where our strength as shepherds will be truly tested. And as we navigate this journey, let's remember to trust in the divine guidance that leads us. To believe in the power of unity and collaboration. To have faith in our people and their capabilities. And to always remember the words of the Holy Spirit and the Scripture that inspire and guide us.

And finally, let's not forget the importance of humility. It is humility that keeps us grounded. It reminds us that while we may be shepherds, we are also part of the flock. It is humility that makes us realize that our success isn't just our own, but a shared success that belongs to all who have contributed to our journey. So, as we continue to build this kingdom, let's keep these principles in mind. Let's strive to make a difference, create a legacy, and shape a business that is not just successful, but also compassionate, inclusive, and reflective of our faith. Together, we can do so much more than we could ever achieve alone. Together, we can build a kingdom, a legacy that will be a testament to our faith, our unity, and our collective effort.

In our previous discussion, we broached the concept of a shepherding movement within your business, a collective effort that transforms the business from being solely an organic expression of your identity to reflecting multiple identities. The #1 question that arises now is: How did this notion make you feel? The prospect can be both unsettling and comforting. The unease could stem from the fear of losing control, from the apprehension of your business morphing into something unrecognizable. Yet, there can also be a sense of peace in the knowledge that your business can be an embodiment of collective experiences, wisdom, and visions.

So, ponder this:

1. *Does the idea of your business becoming an organic expression of not only your identity but also others' identities induce anxiety or tranquility?*

2. *Are you still at ease with following the Holy Spirit's*

guidance in this shared journey?

I urge you to delve into these questions. Communicate your thoughts and feelings in a way that resonates with you and then share the outcome with the people who matter most to you. Is there serenity in the realization that your business could mirror the expressions of various individuals, or does it incite trepidation? And if so, why? What underlying concerns fuel this apprehension? Perhaps, there's a strand of possessiveness threading its way through your emotions. This could manifest as a reluctance to share ownership and control, much like a toddler clutching their favorite toy car, resisting anyone else's touch. This is mine, the internal chant goes, and any challenge to that sense of possession feels threatening. But why is this so? This is a conversation we need to have. The reluctance to share, the apprehension about communal identity – these are concerns we need to lay bare.

Only by bringing these issues into the open can we address them, harness their energy, and purpose them towards a more positive, constructive direction. If we ignore these feelings, they will fester in the shadows, hindering the transformation we're striving for. So, let's bring them into the light. Let's present them before the power of our people, and in doing so, let's find a path towards healing and growth.

CHAPTER 3 - COMMUNICATING
THE LESSER

Before we get deeper into this chapter, let's recap a bit. In our previous sessions, we delved into various topics. In Session One, we highlighted the Power of Pure Communication, the imperative of being present among your team members, and the importance of inviting the Holy Spirit into your business. We also touched upon the symbolic representation of being a Holy Spirit-led king, as the best kings are obedient to the Holy Spirit and also accompanied by prophets. This was an analogy to suggest that as business leaders, significant change-makers and solution-bringers, we need to partner with both the Holy Spirit, and the prophets in business. In Session Two, we expanded the discourse around prophetic business practices and introduced the idea of Prophetic Roundtables. We focused on aligning business strategies around people, not merely systems. The idea of Solutionary Rooms was presented – spaces that allow the voice of God to echo through your business and its people. When the Father designs your business, He does so through people. I termed this phenomenon as the 'Art of Impression', highlighting the creative power of continued design that can be accessed through the impressions made on each of us as we honor and provide space for our people to shine in their gifts and flourish in their unique identities.

Now, as we move to Session Three, we delve deeper into the realm of communication and further explore the concept of a shepherding movement in business. The focal point of today's session is "Communicating the Lesser." You might be wondering what this means - "communicating the lesser." But before we dissect this, let's reflect on the revelations of our earlier conversations. A core belief that has been iterated time and again is the central role people play in any business. The goal is to release solutions through individuals, not confine them within rigid systems.

To illustrate this, I want to reference a verse from the New Testament, 1 Corinthians 14:26: "What then, brothers? When you come together, each one has a hymn, a lesson, a revelation, a tongue, or an interpretation. Let all things be done for building up." Imagine if this principle was applied to your business meetings. Each member contributes their unique insights and perspectives, shares what they are hearing from the Holy Spirit, and all things are done for mutual edification. Could you visualize the transformative impact this would have on the corporate culture, community, and even familial relationships? When the least likely candidate for wisdom is honored, the power that comes through honoring them can create massive opportunity, but we'll never know until we - you guessed it - 'Communicate the Lesser.'

Allow everyone, from your sales team members to the CEO, the freedom to express their ideas, their revelations, their interpretations. Remember, the goal is to foster an environment conducive to growth and development in such a way that brings supernatural increase to the lives of the people you're leading. Then, as a byproduct, your flourishing community of people will produce greater yields, operate in higher wisdom, and even bring the unseen in the seen. (Think: 'Thy Kingdom come, thy will be done, here as it is in heaven.' When we follow the lead of the Holy Spirit, we can bring heaven to earth. That doesn't always look like a sermon. Sometimes it looks like an invention, creation, or exciting new opportunity designed by the Spirit and carried out by you and your people.)

The reason God anointed apostles, prophets, evangelists, pastors, and teachers is for their influence on people and their role in constructing the spiritual body of the church. These eternal principles, when translated into secular settings, can yield enormous benefits. Not by principle alone, but by people who are honored for who they really are. I know many pastors who also have jobs. As employees, they are not regarded as wise, not always approached about the insight God may have for the business, and not honored as a five-fold leader. They wear a pastor hat at the church, but at work they are just an employee in the eyes of their bosses. Imagine the dynamic growth a business could experience when it honors the spiritual mantles placed on the lives of anointed leaders. Your sales person could be a prophet. Your administrative assistant could be anointed to teach. Do you know who your people really are in the eyes of the Father?

The truth remains constant and unchanging. If we make room for the voices of your people and for the voice of the Holy Spirit in your business, imagine the transformation that can occur even in your weakest link. If your weakest link can access the omnipotent wisdom of the Father, that weakness can become a target for the strength of God. When you honor them, it activates their ability to flourish.

It is essential to remember: empowering people is not always about increasing profits. The process of empowerment can yield profit, but it's not the primary goal. Profits are a byproduct of empowering people. The people are the field that you're sowing into. In fostering their growth and development, you are cultivating a fertile field that will yield abundant returns. So, as we move forward, let this key thought guide your approach: Empowering people isn't always about empowering your profits, profits, and ROI are byproducts of pouring into and empowering people.

Remember, people are the field that you sow into, and the harvest you reap will include far more than just money. Let's not overlook the vital truth: seeds produce a harvest. This fact is fundamental, unchangeable. No amount of intentions, concepts, or strategies can bear fruit unless there are seeds planted. Good ideas alone will not suffice. They may be promising, but without seeds, no harvest can be reaped. We can have the greatest ideas, but if we never do anything with them... if we never plant them and water them, no harvest will come from our ideas. If you aspire to see the fruits of a bountiful harvest, you must sow into your field. People around you are your fields, capable of producing a rich harvest. The more individuals you choose to invest in, the more fields you have for the harvest. This is a principle I want to emphasize: every person you invest in by the Spirit, you empower, and they become a fertile field for your harvest. Consider those within your sphere of influence. Maybe it's your team, your colleagues, or your employees. You might see potential brimming, or perhaps you feel the absence of individuals to work with because you haven't made room for them yet. Every person you make room for in your business becomes a vital part of the harvest your business will reap. By providing both the space for them to flourish, and the honor of empowering them, you're unlocking their creative potential, creating a vibrant environment for innovation and expression.

You may be able to quantify the number of people working in your business implementing strategies. But can you count the wealth of profitable business strategies lying dormant within your team simply waiting to be discovered? This concept parallels the familiar analogy of the apple and its seeds. You can easily count the number of seeds in an apple, but can you predict the number of apples that can grow from a single seed? For your business to reach exponential potential, you need to find these seeds within your people and create an environment where they can be planted and nurtured. The fruits that will be yielded for your business will be a direct result of these seeds you've sown. Sowing and reaping is a universal principle, applicable in every sphere, every context.

When you invest in people, when you show them honor and respect, you are sowing seeds for a future harvest. Here's the cop-out: Paying people. This investment in the form of paying them fairly for their time, recognizing their contribution as valuable, and leaving it at that is not what we're talking about here. Honoring them with your money is not honoring them with your interest and desire to see them flourish. So yes, paying them fairly is good, however, mere monetary compensation is not enough. Transition from a transactional relationship to a transformational one. Instead of merely paying for their services, invest in them, sow seeds into them. This seed sowing isn't merely financial; it partners with nurturing, mentoring, guiding – shepherding them.

Some might find this idea unusual. Why would every person who chooses to be a part of my business want to be shepherded? They might not consciously seek it, but in choosing to associate with your business, they are implicitly choosing to be shepherded, because you're the type of leader that builds beyond the basic patterns of traditional business. If you set the example, leading a pastoral reformation in the way you do business, God will reward you with growth. This growth will attract others seeking similar success, creating opportunities for you to advise and mentor, to sow into fields that others will harvest. Competitors will turn to you to find out "how" you're growing, why your people are excited about the work, and more.

At this point, an important question arises. Are you willing to empower other businesses, even at the cost of them possibly reaping greater profits? Does the idea of others learning from your methods and reaping their own harvests cause you peace or anxiety? If the idea instills anxiety, as if these entities are competitors threatening your success, I encourage you to rise above such a scarcity mindset. Remember that you're called to be influential, to provide solutions that catch people's attention, to make a difference. It's inevitable that others will take notice and try to emulate your strategies. And when they do, when they reap their own harvests using your methods, you have a choice to make. You can react out of envy, selfishness, and territoriality, acting like a toddler protective of their toys, or you can embrace your calling as an influencer. If you want to be the one who gets invited to larger stages, meeting rooms, and opportunities, you'll have to push scarcity out of your life.

Jesus illustrated this point with his disciples. He performed miracles, healed the sick, raised the dead, and cast out demons. He then turned to his followers and granted them the authority to do the same in his name. He even sent them out to perform these miracles without him, trusting in their ability to act in his stead. And when they returned with stories of their success, Jesus encouraged them not to marvel at the power they wielded, but to rejoice that their names were written in heaven. Then, he told them that they would continue to do the works that he did, and even greater works! He wasn't ashamed of the fact that they (we) would do greater things. It is his joy as the Good Shepherd to see these things taking place.

Similarly, as you teach and empower your team to enact new heavenly business strategies and witness the success of your business grow, remember not to be amazed solely at the results. Instead, be filled with wonder that you are being used as a vessel, as a conduit for positive change. Be amazed that God trusted you with the strategies for your business, and through your actions, others too are learning and growing. When your work draws attention and your strategies are emulated, don't get caught up solely in the tangible results of your influence. Instead, rejoice that you've been acknowledged by heaven. You are being given strategies and guidance not only for your personal success but to influence others as well.

When others take notice of your methods and implement them, causing their businesses to flourish, take it as a compliment. This is a sign of your influence, a validation of your approach. It's a reminder that your mission is not just about cultivating your own field but about sowing seeds in fields far and wide. The purpose is to create a community that grows and thrives together. So when you see others emulating your strategies, instead of feeling threatened, celebrate it. You're not just building a successful business; you're influencing a successful business culture.

Ok, now let's dive into an incredible portion of Scripture to validate what I'm talking about. Then, I'll break it down for both leading people, and for stewarding products and services. 1 Corinthians 12:14-26 ESV - "For the body does not consist of one member but of many. 15 If the foot should say, "Because I am not a hand, I do not belong to the body," that would not make it any less a part of the body. 16 And if the ear should say, "Because I am not an eye, I do not belong to the body," that would not make it any less a part of the body. 17 If the whole body were an eye, where would be the sense of hearing? If the whole body were an ear, where would be the sense of smell? 18 But as it is, God arranged the members in the body, each one of them, as he chose. 19 If all were a single member, where would the body be? 20 As it is, there are many parts, yet one body. 21 The eye cannot say to the hand, "I have no need of you," nor again the head to the feet, "I have no need of you." 22 On the contrary, the parts of the body that seem to be weaker are indispensable, 23 and on those parts of the body that we think less honorable we bestow the greater honor, and our unpresentable parts are treated with greater modesty, 24 which our more presentable parts do not require. But God has so composed the body, giving greater honor to the part that lacked it, 25 that there may be no division in the body, but that the members may have the same care for one another. 26 If one member suffers, all suffer together; if one member is honored, all rejoice together."

This passage from the Bible is providing a powerful analogy that applies not only to people and communities, but also to businesses. It's reminding us that each person, each role, and each strategy within your business has its place and purpose, no matter how seemingly insignificant or bothersome they might be. Consider the unique strengths, talents, and capacities of each individual in your organization. Every single one of them, from the intern to the CEO, brings something unique to the table. They each embody a different aspect of your business's identity, a different 'member of the body', as it were. Each has a unique function and cannot simply be dismissed because their contribution isn't immediately obvious or because they seem to be underperforming.

The verse suggests that the parts of the body that appear to be weaker are indispensable. This means those who may not be the most vocal, the most obviously talented, or the most visible, are nevertheless vital to the overall function and health of the body. In business terms, these might be the quieter team members, those working behind the scenes, or those working in roles that do not usually get much recognition or attention. They are indispensable because they perform roles that are foundational to the business. They help keep the wheels turning, even if they aren't in the spotlight.

And the passage goes further to state that the parts of the body that we deem as less honorable should be treated with greater honor. This underlines the importance of showing respect and appreciation to those who may not typically receive it, but it doesn't stop there. Honor is much more than general appreciation or respect. It's more than saying "thank you," or hosting a pizza party for the back office staff. Honor truly happens when you make room for their voices, ideas, gifts, and strategies to be heard and stewarded. That doesn't mean everyone gets to do things the way they want to, but it does mean that you're willing to take those ideas and sit with an advisory board of prophets and leaders to weigh the validity of them and implement what is in alignment with the heart of the Father for the business.

In a successful business, every member, every role, every strategy is vital. To create a thriving, inclusive and dynamic business environment, everyone should be valued and appreciated for their unique contributions. Everyone should be honored for what they carry, and most importantly, everyone should have a voice that is recognized and honored just as much as the voice of your strongest link. You don't hear your liver as much as you hear your mouth, but it's a vitally important part to the functionality of your body. This approach in business culture cultivates an atmosphere of mutual respect and teamwork, excitement and wonder, creativity and opportunity, where everyone's voice is acknowledged as being crucial to the overall success of the business.

Moreover, this understanding promotes unity and cooperation within the organization, which is absolutely critical to the overall health of the business. Looking at the end of this passage of Scripture, notice what it says about suffering and honor. If one member suffers, all suffer together. If one member is honored, all rejoice together. This symbiotic relationship is key in fostering a healthy work culture, a successful business, and a thriving community. If you want to teach your business to rejoice, this is one of your keys to making it happen.

Finally, this scripture reminds us that good leadership is about more than just achieving business goals; it's about genuinely caring for and nurturing the people in your organization. Instead of discarding those who are struggling, consider how you might help them to improve, grow, and ultimately thrive. This approach will not only be beneficial for them as individuals, but it will also be beneficial for the overall health and success of your business.

Your business is made up of individuals, each unique in their skills and abilities. These individuals, whether they are your CEO, administrative staff, or coaches, may not necessarily require your immediate attention, especially if they are already performing well and exhibiting exponential growth. However, you must not overlook those struggling within your organization. They might be the ones who need your guidance and assistance the most. The traditional model would have you fire the weakest links and hire new people to fill their spots. To be honest, that's weak. It means you're a thinker but not a leader. You can organize pieces of a puzzle to create a profit, but you aren't even interested in building people or helping them find a path of freedom from their weaknesses. If people are failing under your watch, it's an opportunity to honor, build, and experience radical increase. It's not an opportunity to fire.

Would you fire your kids and kick them out of the house for not being productive, too? Do you burn every relationship that doesn't meet your personal agenda? Is there a trail of broken relationships and failed opportunities behind you everywhere you go because you are unwilling to pour yourself into the people who need you to be present and actually lead? If so, you're a narcissistic leader who needs deliverance and healing. Humble yourself and get help from people who love you, or even find me on social media and send me a message. Past and present failures don't have to dictate your future, but doing nothing about it will never lead to breakthrough.

In any organization, there are always individuals who may be underperforming or may need help. It may seem easier to dismiss these individuals, perhaps even fire them. But as a leader, your role is to shepherd, not to disperse. By investing time and energy in those who are struggling, you are sowing seeds of growth that will yield a harvest. That's what the Word of God says, and it's 100% accurate. Your business is not just about systems and structures; it's about people. Therefore, the identity of your business is an organic expression of the identities of those within it. If an employee's behavior or performance is contrary to what you envision for your business, you should address the issue rather than ignore it. Overlooking such issues could harm the identity of your business, leading to dissonance between the actions of your employees and the goals of your business.

Your role as a leader extends beyond your official duties. It is your responsibility to guide and shepherd your team members, particularly those who are struggling. Failure to do so means missing out on an opportunity to positively influence someone's life.

Ok, let's talk about words.

Words are powerful, and the way we use them can greatly impact the culture and atmosphere of your business. Gossip, for example, is a corrosive force, leading to slander, division, and low morale. If you discover that gossip is prevalent within your organization, it's imperative that you address it immediately. Not only does it disrupt the working environment, but it also tarnishes the identity of your business. Are people gossiping about each other right now in your business? It's time to shepherd them. As a leader, it's crucial to understand that merely recognizing the need to address these issues is not enough. You need to take action. Just as seeds yield a harvest, so do your actions result in change. Until you take action, you won't see any results.

God, in his wisdom, created a body where all parts are important. When you honor and care for each individual in your organization, even those you perceive as weaker or less powerful, it fosters unity and cohesion. If one member of the body suffers, everyone feels it. However, when one member is honored, everyone shares in the joy.

Promoting a culture of honor within your organization can lead to a more harmonious and positive work environment. By honoring even a single person, you can instill a sense of joy and unity that extends to the entire organization. It's not about singling out individuals for praise, but rather fostering an environment where everyone knows that they aren't alone, that their voice is important, and that their failures don't automatically mean termination and disconnection. This promotes a culture of mutual respect and harmony, but it also establishes an environment that fosters real change, real growth, and purposed-compassion which can significantly improve the overall productivity and success of your business.

So remember, as a leader, you are not just managing systems and structures; you are shepherding people. Recognize the value each person brings to your organization and honor them for their contribution. Through your actions, you can create a business that is not just successful, but also a joyous place to flourish alongside leaders who actually care.

Having examined the role of communication, let's pivot towards the core aspect of our enterprise - your business and its products. To fully understand this, let's pull the Scripture back up and read it again.

1 Corinthians 12:14-26 ESV - "For the body does not consist of one member but of many. 15 If the foot should say, "Because I am not a hand, I do not belong to the body," that would not make it any less a part of the body. 16 And if the ear should say, "Because I am not an eye, I do not belong to the body," that would not make it any less a part of the body. 17 If the whole body were an eye, where would be the sense of hearing? If the whole body were an ear, where would be the sense of smell? 18 But as it is, God arranged the members in the body, each one of them, as he chose. 19 If all were a single member, where would the body be? 20 As it is, there are many parts, yet one body. 21 The eye cannot say to the hand,

"I have no need of you," nor again the head to the feet, "I have no need of you." 22 On the contrary, the parts of the body that seem to be weaker are indispensable, 23 and on those parts of the body that we think less honorable we bestow the greater honor, and our unpresentable parts are treated with greater modesty, 24 which our more presentable parts do not require. But God has so composed the body, giving greater honor to the part that lacked it, 25 that there may be no division in the body, but that the members may have the same care for one another. 26 If one member suffers, all suffer together; if one member is honored, all rejoice together."

At King's Company (my business), we've introduced several products over the years. Currently, the Kingdom Life Coaching School is our most popular offering. Inaugurated fully in 2020, it is designed to educate and equip aspiring five-fold leaders who desire to become Kingdom Life Coaches. We equip them in ministry, gifts, identity, spiritual warfare, and more so that they experience massive breakthroughs and can then impart their knowledge to individuals seeking to understand Kingdom life, their gifts and identities, and the Word of God better, too. However, it isn't the only product in our portfolio.

I've authored multiple books, which, in conjunction with the school, form the backbone of our training. One of these books, my debut, is titled 'Prevailing Soul.' Unfortunately, due to a lapsed publishing contract, this book is currently out of print and unavailable for purchase. Such a scenario presents a valuable learning opportunity in understanding our business strategy. Evidently, we have a highly successful arm of our enterprise - the Kingdom Life Coaching School - contrasted with a less successful one, the out-of-print book. This stark difference may tempt us to deprioritize the weaker product, but that is a misguided approach.

Drawing from the Scripture above, conjoined with the analogy of the human body, no organ can dismiss another's importance. Just like the eye cannot claim that it doesn't need the hand, our coaching school cannot dismiss 'Prevailing Soul.' Conversely, 'Prevailing Soul' cannot declare its independence from the coaching school. Regardless of how we perceive them, the seemingly weaker parts are indispensable. Yes, I'm talking about products in my business needing to be honored like parts of the body.

This principle extends to our business. We must honor our less successful products, not because they will suddenly become bestsellers, but because they are part of our business body. The value they bring extends beyond immediate profits; they contribute to our brand, influence, and overall business narrative. Take a moment and consider what products, services, or creations you currently have in your arsenal. Which ones are weaker? Which ones are flourishing? In practical terms, we can equate this to the marketing strategy for our coaching school. We run sponsored ads on Facebook and Instagram, which successfully draw individuals to live events, courses, coaching, and ultimately the school. However, focusing only on our successful product neglects the principle of giving greater honor to the part that lacks it, which in this case is the 'Prevailing Soul' book.

The lack of 'Prevailing Soul' in the market signifies division in our business body. To rectify this, we must bestow greater honor to it, thereby eliminating division and ensuring all parts of the business receive the same attention, even when they don't serve the same purposes. Just like we honor the voice of the intern as much as the voice of the lead sales team member, in business we should honor the products and services in our business with wisdom. This approach brings us to a remarkable revelation. Even though our business is experiencing tremendous growth, it's not yet rejoicing. Why? Because one member is suffering. If the Prevailing Soul continues to suffer; the whole business suffers. But if it is honored, the whole business will rejoice. We have yet to tap into our full potential, indicating that there's more growth and success awaiting us.

Noticing the neglect of 'Prevailing Soul' made me question other areas of my business that might also be overlooked. However, instead of becoming overwhelmed by the task of identifying all such areas, I realized that all it takes is honoring one part of the business. By bringing 'Prevailing Soul' back to the market, we honor it, sparking joy across the entire company. The aim is not about how many books we sell, but about honoring each product, each member of our business. When you understand this, you realize that profit is just a byproduct of a balanced, harmonious business strategy. Recognizing the Holy Spirit's work in your business isn't just about empowering profits; sometimes, it's about sowing into your products to reap a holistic harvest.

In the beginning, I stated that empowering people isn't always about empowerment. That profit is a secondary outcome, and the individuals that form your team are the fertile ground that you nourish. However, this principle also extends to your products. Empowering your products isn't purely about increasing profit. Once again, profit is a byproduct, and your product is the fertile field you invest in. The point isn't to develop strategies to earn a significant sum of money from a book. You've misunderstood the premise if that's what you thought. Instead, my focus is on formulating a strategy that honors the book. The goal is to respect the creative endeavor, and in doing so, something like my Kingdom Life Coaching School may witness exponential sales. It'll rejoice, not because of the financial gain, but because the book was accorded the honor it needed.

This brings me to an important question: how does one go about doing this?

My approach to growth is often to take to Facebook, where I post a series of inspirational messages, educational content, and revelation pieces, plus run paid ads to bring people into an opportunity for growth, education, coaching, or similar. However, at the time I started receiving this revelation of honoring business products, I noticed that about eight consecutive posts were urging people to join us for one singular event: the Five-fold Challenge. It became clear that this was not only tedious but also led me to neglect other aspects of my business during that time. Despite its repetitive nature, this product managed to draw over 5500 individuals into the 5-day training program within two months, leading to successful live events and generating nearly half a million in revenue in just those two months.

This experience made me realize that I could take the same route for other offerings. Why couldn't I use a similar strategy for something like the Prevailing Soul on my Facebook page? Perhaps I could hire a graphic designer to create graphics that honor the product, and a copywriter to describe it in the divine language given to me. The subsequent step would be to assign this task to them and use the created content to honor the book over the following twelve weeks. Whether or not I led people from the book to the school, it didn't matter. I could do that, but even if I didn't, the book would still be honored.

This approach would lead my business to rejoice for a simple reason: what was once perceived as a weak but indispensable member of the business portfolio is now receiving the recognition it deserved. Instead of allowing one product to suffer, leading the entire business to suffer, we can now have one product celebrated, leading all to rejoice. So, I did it. I started pushing the book in simple posts. Get this... within 2-3 months, I took on multiple consulting clients in a new industry I hadn't even tapped into yet. I had 9 new Health and Wellness Coaches and Functional Medicine Practitioners suddenly hire me. I didn't even know I was called to lead those people.

This is the essence of "communicating the lesser." It's a revelation we need in our businesses. It's not only about improving our people and profits but also about enhancing our products and the culture we build around them. We're here with a purpose: to make a difference in the world. Why shouldn't we strive to make that difference through every facet of our business? The product you offer shouldn't just be a commodity; it should be a tool for healing and rejuvenation, increase and abundance, opportunity and strategy for you, your teams, and even your customers and clients.

So, I pose this question to you: will you "Communicate the Lesser?" Will you learn to honor the least presentable individual or product in your business or community? Will you lead with wisdom and compassion to unleash and activate Rejoicing in your business?

As we wrap up Chapter 3, let's ponder upon these questions:

1. Are you willing to communicate the lesser, in a manner that uplifts people rather than breaking them down?

2. Are you ready to disrupt and eliminate all gossip and slander within your business?

3. How significant is the identity of your weakest link, both in terms of people and products?

These questions aren't mere exercises; they are necessary steps for building a culture of communication deep within your heart. If it is through communication that you can truly see your business flourish. Will you accept the challenge to go further?

Intermission: Soaking in Eternal
Strategies for Your Business

I hope this has been an exciting continuation of your leadership journey so far. This section's discussion carries forward with a recap of what we've covered so far. The reason I do this is because a little repetition will help you soak up the principles in your heart. The better you understand them, the better you will operate in them!

In our first session, we spoke about the power of trust. We delved into how uncertainty about navigating trust could hinder the development of mutually synergistic relationships, constraining your potential for growth. I emphasized the significance of proximity—how sharing the same physical space could facilitate pure communication, enabling you to establish and deepen trust. Spending time with people, making deposits into and withdrawals from the 'trust bank' as guided by the Spirit, can help foster stronger bonds. We also tackled the seemingly intimidating task of hearing God's voice. I reassured you that the ability to hear God isn't exclusive to believers or spiritual veterans —it's an innate gift we all possess. The Holy Spirit has been poured out on all of us; all we need to do is to attune ourselves to His guidance.

We discussed the dangers of deception, an art that our enemy has perfected. When we allow ourselves to be led by the world's standards or the enemy's manipulations, we're at risk of straying from the path that God intends for us, a path that leads to the best possible outcome for us and our businesses.

We reflected on the distinct timelines of the earthly world and eternity, highlighting how the former has a clear beginning and end while the latter is infinite. By learning to communicate with God in our business endeavors, we gain access to an eternal inheritance, an eternal wisdom that isn't bound by earthly patterns or limitations.

The first session concluded with the idea that we were all created to unlock the 'hidden code' of eternity in our business operations. We're called to exert dominion over the darkness and bring forth supernatural solutions to the problems birthed in it. This transformative shift in perspective is vital to the implementation of an eternal strategy in life and business. The Holy Spirit, our Helper and Guide, provides us with the keys to this transformative power that transcends the bounds of earthly timelines. If you still feel disconnected from the Holy Spirit, I urge you to seek the company of someone who is attuned to its voice, allowing you to reap the benefits indirectly.

We discussed the power of inviting the prophetic into your business, transforming it into an altar where you offer your endeavors to God. The fire that God sends down not only purifies but also illuminates your path. Proverbs 25:2 reminds us that it is our glory, as kings and queens, to seek out the mysteries that God has hidden. In doing so, we step into our spheres of influence, offering solutions and meeting needs. We touched upon the significance of respect and recognition. The more we honor others, the more their true identities are revealed, inviting them to step into their own mantles from God, distributed with power and eternal authority—the anointing. This anointing is amplified and transferred when we engage with others. The session culminated with the importance of asking the right questions, for questions make room for answers, creating opportunity for holy communications.

In session two, we moved onto the art of impression and being marked by the Creator's design. God continues to shape us through the people we interact with. His divine blueprint for our actions and ambitions is revealed to us through the community we build. This ties into the power of unity, of acknowledging others, and providing room for their voices. We delved into the concept of pastoral reformation—a shepherding movement in every industry. A business that nurtures a shepherding culture will reap the benefits of this spiritual sowing. When people of God, led by the Spirit of God, engage with others, they imprint the marks of the Divine Designer on all members of the community. Through a pastoral or shepherding approach, we can facilitate not just business growth, but transformative change in people's lives.

In session two, we discussed the need for inclusive spaces in our businesses. Every voice should be welcomed and heard. This led us to the concepts of prophetic roundtables and solutionary rooms, two innovative approaches to fostering collaboration and communication in a spiritual business environment. Solutionary rooms could be identified as war rooms, strategy rooms, visionary rooms, innovation rooms, the inventor's table, or Kingdom life discussions. In essence, they are gatherings of minds focused on a single business sphere, all with one objective: to listen for the strategies of heaven. For instance, if our marketing tactics need refinement, we create a space specifically to discern divine marketing strategies.

As we navigate these sessions together, my hope is that we continue to learn, grow, and harness the power of God's personal wisdom in our businesses. This journey is as much about our personal and spiritual growth as it is about our professional development. And remember, regardless of where you find yourself right now, the Holy Spirit is always accessible, ready to guide you in both life and business. So, let us step into the next stage of our journey together, carrying with us the lessons we've learned and the truths we've uncovered. In our upcoming sessions, we'll continue to unravel God's plan for us and our businesses, bridging the gap between the earthly and the eternal, and moving ever closer towards a business strategy that is not only successful but also spiritually fulfilling.

In these discussions, it has been stressed that a business is not a sterile, isolated construct, but an organic extension of its constituents' identities. Initially, your venture mirrors your own persona. However, when you begin to respect and celebrate those who comprise your workforce, your enterprise evolves to reflect their identities as well. This perspective raises some fundamental questions, particularly concerning the impact on your peace of mind and anxiety levels when your business begins to personify the collective identity of its workforce, rather than just yours.

Fundamentally, it is about creating a Shepherding movement, which brings about supernatural growth in your business. In refusing to embrace this movement, you run the risk of building a self-centric, rather than a community-centric venture. The process is effort-driven; one must take the lead, committing to nurture others, fueling your business with their enthusiasm and drive. The ultimate reward is a business defined by the solutions it provides and distinguished by the individuals it empowers.

The quest for influence is vital. The greater the growth of our businesses, the more influence we can exert in our respective sectors. Influence, however, is born out of the creator's design manifested through people. A business must therefore, prioritize its people because therein lies its true potential for growth. Failing to recognize this would result in missed opportunities. These beliefs have guided us into our third session where we dove into the lesser known aspects of our businesses and appreciated the power they wield. Everyone engaged in your enterprise must understand your aspiration to implement a Shepherding movement in your business. This is more than a business—it's a business that values people, guided by the principles of care and honor. Each person involved needs to grasp your vision and perceive the divine heart of your business.

We've underscored that the strength of a business correlates to your willingness to uplift the weakest link until it radiates vibrantly. This involves devoting more of your efforts to the lesser presentable parts of your venture so the more presentable parts can thrive independently. The driving principle is straightforward: seeds bring about harvest, not mere intentions, concepts, or even courses. The content of this course will yield a bounty only if you diligently apply it to your business.

In the third session, we asserted that empowering people is not tantamount to empowering profits. Profit growth is a happy consequence of the growth of your people. They are the fertile fields you sow into, and the more you invest in them, the more fields become available for harvest. Any neglect or dishonor meted out to a weaker part of the business body leads to discord, which causes collective suffering. Conversely, when one member is celebrated, all rejoice together. This principle extends to the products your business offers as well. The concept of disregarding any product, irrespective of its sales figures, is unproductive. Each product, even those that seem weaker, are indispensable and warrant our respect and care. It's a business truism: if one product suffers, it's felt across the entire business. If one product is celebrated, it evokes collective joy.

That wraps up the summary of our first three sessions.

Let's move into session four, which revolves around "Strategies for Every Need." If you're prepared to dive into divine strategies for all your business needs, then feel free to express your enthusiasm by jotting down a note of agreement in your notepad, something along the lines of, "I am ready to embrace divine strategies for every business need I have."

It's essential to understand that today marks a significant departure from solely relying on human solutions or even ones you've personally devised. This shift is essential because to tap into the realm of the supernatural, to experience extraordinary growth in your business, you must be willing to transcend your own limitations, including the confines of your intellect and logic.

Consider this: if your strategies and overall understanding of business can be easily dissected and comprehended within your intellect, then it is not supernatural; it is simply natural. If you grasp the entirety of what is happening in your enterprise without any sense of wonder or mystery, it's likely not a supernatural phenomenon. To truly venture into the supernatural, we must be willing to operate outside our own abilities. This means moving into a realm where success is "exceedingly abundantly beyond anything we can ask or think." In this venture, we aren't left completely in the dark; we are part of the process, learning and understanding as we move along. However, there will be moments when we'll question certain aspects of the process. Times when we won't fully comprehend why a particular strategy is effective. In these moments, it's crucial to remember that your understanding is not a prerequisite for success. God's ways and thoughts are far superior to ours.

If we aspire to conduct our businesses in line with divine creative design and to utilize eternal strategies that foster growth, we must be prepared to take risks that might seem daunting from a human perspective. This risk-taking is not a reckless plunge into the unknown, but a calculated step into a realm of spiritual power and growth. We must trust in divine guidance and open ourselves to opportunities and possibilities beyond our natural comprehension.

CHAPTER 4: STRATEGIES FOR EVERY NEED

Diving headfirst into this dialogue, the primary focus becomes the idea of vision. Vision, as the guiding light for any business, is essential. If you don't have a holistic vision for your business already, it's high time you carve out time to do so. If your enterprise is branching out with a new income stream or exploring a new business avenue, it's equally essential to cultivate a vision for each new direction you take. These visions should be clear, comprehensible, and most importantly, written down.

This stems from a Scripture rooted in the Book of Habakkuk - make the vision plain, write it down so that those who read it can run with it. As a business leader, the people under your guidance need to comprehend the business's heart and vision. They must understand the essence of the business as they shepherd and steward it. Although the business will be an organic expression of their individual identities too, it will primarily be birthed through leaders who are chosen and instilled with a specific calling to reach people.

God has bestowed upon you a unique mantle of authority to meet needs and provide solutions to worldly problems. If your team doesn't fully grasp your vision, they cannot effectively carry it out. You have been called to leadership for a reason. You are not an employee but the pioneer and forerunner of this venture. It's vital that your team comprehends this. If they see the vision, they can run with it. The Lord may supplement it through them, providing them with the guidelines and restrictions that aid and steer.

Interestingly, there's a verse in Proverbs 29:18 that asserts, "Where there is no prophetic vision, the people cast off restraint, but blessed is he who keeps the law." This tells us that with prophetic vision, we set boundaries and restrictions that are beneficial for us. Operating within the confines of this vision is where the power lies. Straying outside the vision will only hinder your progress. When you can discern what lies within the vision, you can simultaneously identify what is outside of it. This allows you to pursue the vision and sideline all external distractions.

The paramount question that arises then is - How do we approach God for answers in our business? There are two categories to delve into here: learning to listen and learning to seek. It's okay if this feels new. Newness doesn't inherently denote badness. New experiences can breathe life into hope, excitement, and joy. As we navigate these fresh waters, there is scope for deception, but there is also room for growth, discernment, and developing your gifts in an unstoppable fashion. So, instead of shying away from what's new, embrace it, learn from it, grow with it.

In your business, you will need solutionary rooms to increase and develop better strategies in each business area. To make this happen, you will have to set the meeting, invite people to it, and have the meeting. During these meetings, you will need to learn to listen and to seek. God communicates in ways we are receptive to. So, if you are questioning how God might speak to you, remember this - He will do it in ways that either resonate with you or grab your attention. He is willing to speak to you in the ways that you learn to listen.

God is more than a divine entity; he is also a Father. Therefore, his guidance won't merely be managerial; he will nurture you along the way. So, you must learn to listen and seek. This course might be the path through which God captures your attention and instigates a more intimate conversation with Him. The ultimate goal here is not just to know about God or the Bible, but to know God as a person and embrace the One who sent his own Son to be sacrificed for our lives.

Jesus, having risen from the dead and ascended into heaven, is alive and still communicative. His earthly existence isn't a barrier to his continued connection with us. His promises remain true and accessible; his life force resonates through the world even today. Indeed, his life and teachings are not a relic of the past but an ongoing, unfolding story that invites us into communion and co-creation. We are co-heirs with Christ, and we have direct access to the Lord, at any time, for any reason. You can hear His voice, you can know His thoughts for you. This underlines the fact that he didn't just leave behind a message or a book, but he made a path for us to follow, a way of life for us to embrace. He's not a silent, absentee figure but a tangibly present person in relationship with us who is capable of guiding us in our business ventures, too. It's a matter of learning to listen for his voice, of seeking his guidance actively, and of developing the faith and trust that he will guide us.

Listening to Jesus in our business practices is not about straining to hear an audible voice from heaven. Instead, it's about developing an attentive spirit that can discern his guidance in our thoughts, in the circumstances around us, and in the insights and wisdom shared by others who follow the leading of the Holy Spirit too. We don't need a grand, supernatural event to hear from God. Instead, we need a humble and open heart that is willing to seek and listen.

The first of the two categories that we should focus on is learning to listen. This is not just about hearing words but discerning the voice of God amid the noise of life. It's about perceiving the divine nudge in our hearts, recognizing the sense of peace that comes when we're moving in the right direction, and developing the spiritual intuition to understand when something is from God. This can be constructive, nurturing, mending, or even corrective, but anything he speaks to us is authoritative and true. Revere Him and reap the reward. Next, we need to learn to seek. Seeking God for answers in our business does not mean we expect to find an easy solution for every problem. Rather, it's about seeking his will, his guidance, and his wisdom in every situation. It's about aligning our plans with his purposes, striving to build businesses that reflect his Kingdom values, and seeking to serve others in ways that demonstrate his love and justice.

In our businesses, creating these solutionary rooms for seeking and listening becomes imperative. Ideas alone do not generate results; it's the seeds sown through diligent effort that yield a harvest. You must take the initiative, set up the meeting, invite people to it, and execute it. Only through such concrete steps can we begin to listen, to seek, and to align our businesses with God's vision.

The voice of God is not reserved for the past or limited to the pages of Scripture. It is a living voice that speaks to us today, even in the context of our businesses. As business leaders, we are called not just to manage but to steward, not just to produce profits but to produce good fruits that bless others and honor God. And in this mission, we can be assured that we are not alone. We have the promise of Jesus, the guidance of the Holy Spirit, and the everlasting love of God the Father accompanying us every step of the way.

Solutionary Rooms:

Initiate what we call 'solutionary rooms'—gatherings focused on active listening and intentional dialogue. The aim is to discern God's voice in our business conversations, strategies, and decisions. For instance, when discussing a marketing strategy, pause and create space for silence. Ask your team, "Is there anything that God might want to add or take away from this?" Allow time and space for everyone to listen. You might be surprised by the insights that emerge during this moment of silence. It might feel awkward initially, but over time, this will yield fresh perspectives, creative solutions, and even course corrections. Encourage your team to share their impressions, even if they seem vague or hard to understand. If a consensus doesn't emerge, don't worry. Perhaps the strategy is good as it gets. But if someone suggests a significant change, based on their discernment, consider it seriously. You might even test the proposed change alongside the original strategy, comparing results to determine which approach performs better. But, in the end, it's not about how you compare strategies, it's about how to trust the voice of the Father in your business.

Partner with People Who Hear God's Voice:

You don't have to do this alone. Partner with people who are sensitive to God's voice. These could be friends, spiritual leaders, or mentors with a proven track record of listening to and being led by God. I have raised up many five-fold leaders, including prophets, who are ready, willing, and able to come alongside you in your business. If you don't have anyone who operates like this, just reach out to me and ask me for some prophets. Seriously, I'll send them your way. Consider John 10:27, where Jesus says, "My sheep listen to my voice; I know them, and they follow me." Surround yourself with 'sheep'—those who know how to listen to the Shepherd's voice.

Lean Into His Voice Yourself:

Listening to God isn't an ability reserved for certain spiritual elites. You, too, can learn to discern His voice. Consider setting aside time for focused listening. For example, put the kids to bed a little early one night, retreat to a quiet place, and give yourself a half-hour of uninterrupted silence. You'll find that God wants to speak to you, and you'll discover that your own personal desire to hear from Him will grow.

Choose a topic—perhaps a business problem or a relationship challenge—and ask God to speak into that situation. Ask questions, let Him answer. Share your thoughts and feelings with Him, then sit quietly and listen. Write down any thoughts, images, or impressions that come to mind, even if they seem unrelated or distracting. Sometimes, what seems like a distraction might be the Holy Spirit highlighting something significant in a way that only you will understand. After this time of listening, review your notes. Highlight what feels relevant and cross out what seems irrelevant. Ask the Holy Spirit for confirmation: "Did I understand correctly?" and "What do you want me to do with this?"

This process may involve repentance—a change of heart that leads to a change of mind, which in turn leads to a change of action. Repentance is not just an expression of regret; it's a commitment to a new direction, an openness to being reshaped by

God's guidance. As you follow these steps—initiating solutionary rooms, partnering with others, and learning to listen to yourself—you'll find yourself developing a more discerning spirit and a more attentive heart. You'll become more proficient at distinguishing God's voice amid the noise of life. And this will not only deepen your spiritual life but will also enhance your business strategies, relationships, and results. Before you know it, you'll be engaged in ongoing dialogue with God, a two-way conversation that enriches your business, your relationships, and your life. And all it takes is one successful engagement to build your confidence in your ability to hear the Holy Spirit's voice in your business.

Continuing on the subject of learning to listen, we're moving towards the fourth point - Learning his language and character from the Word of God. An important note, which may spark some disagreement among traditionalists, is that you don't necessarily have to pick up the King James Version of the Bible. While it carries historical importance, its language can be challenging to comprehend. The English Standard Version is another alternative, as it offers a language style more attuned to modern English, plus it's more accurate than the KJV when compared to Septuagint texts. Whichever translation you decide to study, the primary goal is to immerse yourself in God's Word. As you do, you will gain a greater understanding of His character and manner of communication.

Now, it's essential to approach this process with patience. There might be passages that seem difficult to grasp at first. Instead of letting that frustrate you, continue reading. The seeds of understanding are being sown, and with time, their meaning will become apparent. If you are unsure about which book to start with, ask for guidance from the Holy Spirit. Reach out to someone well-versed in the Scriptures if you have questions or need clarification. The more you familiarize yourself with the Bible, the more discerning you will become in distinguishing the voice of the Holy Spirit from deceptive voices.

Having covered the aspect of 'learning to listen', let's now delve into 'learning to seek'. The concept here is like the 'solutionary rooms', except we are now focusing on visionary rooms. In this setting, we're shifting from spiritually perceiving ideas to visually conceptualizing them. You might find this more engaging if you're a visual person, like me. I see things in the Spirit, able to visualize spiritual narratives and concepts vividly. Consider this: when I describe a red balloon to you, most of you would be able to picture it in your mind's eye. If I then suggest changing the balloon's color to blue, green, or yellow, your imagination follows suit. This innate ability to see, even with your eyes open, is a testament to the divine power that enables us to perceive visually in the Spirit.

Seeing in the Spirit is NOT seeing spiritually. Let me make myself clear when I tell you that seeing spiritually can be the work of the enemy as much as it is a gift from the Father. Stay away from witchcraft, sorcery, divination, and the new age. Those things are NOT holy, beneficial, or healthy. They will lead you right into perversion of this ability and destroy your life from the inside out. Don't make things up, force imaginations, or step into practices that aren't rooted in the Word of God. I promise if you lean into the Holy Spirit, you will go further spiritually than any witchcraft, divination, or new age practice can ever take you. Plus, you won't have to deal with demons, covenants with fallen angels, and the spiritual warfare that comes with doing unholy things. I know this paragraph is crazy, but just trust me on this one. I'm protecting you from experiencing hell on earth, financial and business attacks, and attacks on your family.

There will be people who find seeing in the Spirit in a holy way a bit unusual or dismiss it as fantasy, but I can attest to the significant role it has played in my personal and professional life. Many strategies that have driven my business success have originated from these spiritual visualizations. As a leader, God has provided clarity and reason to my actions through these visual insights. I believe I have a mandate to impart this ability to see and hear in the Spirit. Hopefully, through my teachings, you may also ignite your own capability to perceive in this profound manner.

Let's dive into the concept of visionary rooms. Just imagine gathering a group of people in a room to discuss a specific topic or to address a struggle for which a solution is needed. Why are these people here? Because together we can listen, together we can look. The intent is to invite individuals who are visionary, those who can perceive what is not seen with the physical eye. Along with these visionaries, we bring in prophets who can listen to the Spirit. Once they've gathered, we create an environment conducive to open and creative dialogue. The prophets keep us safe because they know the difference between the real and the fake. They know the difference between the Father's instruction and the error of the devil's deceit.

In this setting, we might take a moment of silence to listen and observe what transpires within the room. It could be a physical space adorned with a whiteboard where everyone is invited to express their thoughts and ideas visually. We might even hand out crayons and markers, encouraging everyone to tap into their creativity. Allow this creative process to flow freely for about 20 to 30 minutes, and who knows what might emerge from it.

Now, this may sound too playful or childish, and here's where I want to clarify something. We tend to outgrow our childhood joys and the carefree nature of our younger selves due to societal expectations and personal responsibilities. As adults, we might wake up, missing the excitement of playing with toys, drawing with colors, or simply letting our imagination run wild. Our creativity, instead of being a tool for expression, is often sidelined as child's play, and we are urged to move on to more "serious" matters. However, it is crucial to understand that we are intended to be like little children even as adults. This doesn't imply being childish, but being childlike, embracing creativity and incorporating a sense of fun in life and business.

You might question the practicality of this approach. But let's loosen up a bit. We don't want to play with fire, but we do want to play with creativity. Why not book a retreat by the beach, invite people over, and blast your favorite worship songs as you collectively seek guidance from the Holy Spirit for your business? What's wrong with incorporating crayons or any other elements that encourage creative expression and facilitate fun? It's ok to have fun in your business suit, I promise. In addition, I urge you to consider partnering with dream interpreters, dreamers, and seers who listen to the Holy Spirit. However, a word of caution – avoid individuals who claim to have spirit guides or angels guiding them. They are not operating within the kingdom of God. As real as these spiritual occurrences might be, they do not possess divine authority or power to guide you towards your intended destination. If people are more excited about angels than they are the Holy Spirit, get them out of your presence. Even if they claim to be Christians, they are highly deceived.

Therefore, prioritize seeking the companionship of dreamers, interpreters, and seers who listen to the Holy Spirit and walk in righteousness. This is the first step towards establishing visionary rooms, which in turn, promote creativity and playful exploration. Encourage collective daydreaming with God, allowing Him to show you things beyond the conventional. He might take you on a spiritual journey through a garden, a high mountain peak, or a field of lavender, revealing symbolic meanings that can be applied to your situation. Trust the voice of the Father that you've become familiar with through His Word. (The Bible) As you mature in your relationship with Him, you might find that He initiates the conversation, bringing in remarkable strategies for your business through dreams, visions, and supernatural unctions that come upon your people.

A final exhortation from this dialogue: Learn symbolism directly from the Holy Spirit and not the Internet. It's essential to understand that what the Holy Spirit shows you, He is willing to explain. This will enable you to avoid misunderstandings and anxiety in your relationship with Him. So, in learning to seek divine guidance, remember these four steps: create visionary rooms, partner with Prophets, holy dream interpreters, righteous seers, and be willing to daydream with God, and learn to understand the symbolism that comes to you from the Holy Spirit. Reject new age, witchcraft, divination, sorcery, enchantments, and anything that isn't coming straight from the mouth of your Father in heaven!

Through this approach, you will unlock new Kingdom realities, strategies, and protocols in your business and you will experience supernatural growth. Remember, everything holy has a counterfeit. Just because the enemy created a weak, ineffective version of something holy doesn't mean the holy version should be discounted. The Bible, the inherent Word of God, is FULL of examples of leaders, kings, and business owners partnering with revelation that comes through hearing, seeing, dreaming, and understanding what the Lord is saying.

We're going to dive deeper into the spiritual journey and understand how it ties into your business. Let's debunk one of the major misconceptions that we have about God - the idea that He's somewhere up there in the heavens and we are down here, detached and disconnected from Him. It's a lie. When Jesus ascended to heaven, He promised us the Holy Spirit, an embodiment of God, to guide us here on earth. He said, "I will not leave you as orphans, I will come to you, and I will manifest myself to you" So, even though the Father and Jesus are in heaven and physically seem "out of reach", the Holy Spirit is here on earth, guiding us into all truth. This truth is the presence of God; this truth is Jesus because He is the way, the truth, and the life.

So, you might wonder, how does this tie into our business? Did we just step into church? Ephesians 2:6 tells us that we are already seated with Christ in heavenly places. Our spirits aren't bound by the earthly realm. Instead, they have access to the heavenly domain, where eternity is accessed, and righteousness resides. This is where our spiritual intelligence, our divine strategies for daily life and business, originate. You were born for something greater. You desire to move in power, and I understand that because I do too. This is the way to access the supernatural power you were born to lead with. It's in your Father, it's through the Spirit, and you have access because of Jesus. Dismiss any religious jargon that opposes this truth, because if you read the Bible in its entirety for yourself, you'll quickly realize that you've been lied to most of your life about spiritual things, even if you grew up in the church. Stop seeing yourself as the broken sinner, and start seeing yourself as a son or daughter of God that all creation is groaning to see revealed.

With this understanding, we need to realize that God never intended us to be separate from Him. His plan was always for us to be close, to be in constant communication with Him. In fact, we are invited into the throne room of Heaven. It may seem wild, but it's the truth. When we gain access to the heavenly realm through faith in the sacrifice of Jesus, all of Heaven celebrates. This celebration doesn't just stop with us; it extends to our businesses as well. (By the way, if your life is getting wrecked by the presence of the Holy Spirit as you read this, and you've never given your life to Christ, PLEASE reach out to me. I will walk you through this process of accepting salvation and will find a place for you to be baptized in water. Welcome to the life you were born to experience. Welcome to salvation. Please reach out even if you're a bit scared. I want to talk with you personally and help you thrive in your journey of true fullness of life in Christ.)

Why does this matter for your business? I believe that if you learn to rejoice in God's presence, your business will also experience this joy. Your willingness to shepherd your business towards God is key. A shepherd's heart seeks to nurture and protect the flock, much like how a business leader nurtures and protects their business.

In the Scripture, Jesus tells a parable of a shepherd who leaves the ninety-nine sheep to find the one lost sheep. He doesn't rest until he finds it, and once he does, he rejoices. Not just him, his friends, his neighbors, and all of Heaven rejoice with him. This joy in Heaven is greater over one sinner who repents and steps into the glory of God than over ninety-nine righteous persons who think they need no repentance. This is the shepherd's heart that God is encouraging us to have for our businesses. Just like a shepherd cares for each individual sheep, as a business leader, you need to care for every aspect of your business. God is the great Shepherd, and He will guide us in this process, showing us how to shepherd our businesses effectively.

Now, let's talk about treasures. We all want to build treasures, have influence, and do well in our businesses. But where are we laying up these treasures? The scripture instructs us not to lay up treasures on earth where they can be destroyed but in heaven. The more we focus on earthly treasures, the more we limit ourselves. However, if we lay up treasures in heaven, we gain access to the Creator of things.

How do we access these heavenly treasures for our business? The answer lies in people and relationships. There are business strategies in relationships with people that can unlock financial withdrawals from heaven for your business. The more time you spend with people, the more heavenly treasure you can withdraw for your business. Don't believe me? Try to prove me wrong. Do your due diligence and start pouring yourself into people and then come tell me if it doesn't work. You'll be coming to tell me it DID work, and not only did you build better relationships, your business flourished. I double dog dare you to give it a shot.

Finally, let's talk about vision. The scripture says the eye is the lamp of the body. If your eye is healthy, your whole body is full of light, but if it's bad, your body is full of darkness. Similarly, if we have our spiritual eyes open we can see divine strategies for our business. However, if our eyes are closed, we limit ourselves to the darkness, forgetting what the light looks like. It's time to open our spiritual eyes and see the things of the Spirit so that we can implement divine strategies in our business. Let's cast off the junk, invite better things, and bring in divine eternal strategies into our business operations. That's what we're striving for in this present moment.

This is the question: Can divine eternal strategies bring us financial abundance? Indeed, they can. However, our path to such financial prosperity was not without its own unique challenges. It was our commitment and obedience to the Holy Spirit that guided us to our current state. We approached God with a specific, heartfelt reverence, and we embraced a process of loving on people that was crucial to our journey. It's an enlightening realization, isn't it? But yes, financial abundance came. I remember making $1200 every two weeks and praying for a breakthrough because I didn't know how to feed my family. Now, I remember times where I brought in $110k in two months, or had $10k days in my business (many times). The Father will take care of those who take care of His people and show them the love He has for them. That's not Scripture, but it's what I believe and have experienced along my own journey of expansion.

Matthew 6:24 "No one can serve two masters, for either he will hate the one and love the other, or he will be devoted to the one and despise the other. You cannot serve God and money."

In the next passage of scripture, we're warned that no one can serve two masters. For one will invariably hate one and love the other, or they will be devoted to one and despise the other. We are reminded that we cannot serve both God and money. Now, consider this. Have you seen people in your life who have shown great devotion to money while ignoring or even despising God? I certainly have, and it is their prerogative to make such a choice. They have every right to reject God and turn away. However, let me tell you that this does not seem logical to me. The price for your ability to choose, to access eternal hope, has already been paid. Why would anyone turn their back on that?

I didn't. I embraced it, and it is because of this acceptance that I am here, advocating for our right to boldly approach the throne of grace to receive mercy and grace in our times of need. This isn't about giving our lives to God in the hope of some future redemption. It's so much more than that. It's about the fact that God has already paid the ultimate price so that he could be with us here, teaching us to emulate His ways.

The Bible speaks of a time when if we learn to steward the things of the Kingdom on earth, we will be entrusted with cities. This isn't about reincarnation, but a time when this heaven and earth will cease to exist, and a new heaven, a new earth, a new Jerusalem will be established. We will spend eternity with God on this new earth, in new physical bodies. Despite its significance, this message often goes unshared, a fact I find perplexing. God encourages us to boldly approach the throne of grace to receive mercy and grace in times of need. This isn't merely a personal need but extends to the needs of your business as well. This is not a suggestion but a command, an imperative. God's intent is not for us to stay in a submissive, falsely humble state, but rather to approach him, for he has an inheritance for us.

Matthew 11:25-30 ESV "At that time Jesus declared, "I thank you, Father, Lord of heaven and earth, that you have hidden these things from the wise and understanding and revealed them to little children; 26 yes, Father, for such was your gracious will. 27 All things have been handed over to me by my Father, and no one knows the Son except the Father, and no one knows the Father except the Son and anyone to whom the Son chooses to reveal him. 28 Come to me, all who labor and are heavy laden, and I will give you rest. 29 Take my yoke upon you, and learn from me, for I am gentle and lowly in heart, and you will find rest for your souls. 30 For my yoke is easy, and my burden is light."

He prompts us to lay up these things in our hearts and bring them to pass on earth. This isn't about receiving a paternal pat on the head. It's about receiving divine strategy that can transform the world, even amidst your struggles. He also offers comfort, inviting all who are weary and burdened to find rest in him. Now, consider this passage. Jesus declared his thanks to the Father, Lord of Heaven and Earth, for hiding things from the wise and understanding and revealing them to little children. This verse takes us back to our earliest, most innocent selves, urging us to rediscover our creativity and our bond with God. It tells us that some things are hidden, not from us, but for us, and to access them, we must become like little children.

God intends to transfer wealth from the wicked to the righteous, and this shift will largely be fueled by those willing to unearth what has been hidden from the wise and reveal it with childlike faith and enthusiasm. Jesus goes on to affirm that it was God's will to do this and that all things have been entrusted to him by his Father. It was his choice to reveal it to the world. Jesus extends an invitation to those who labor and are heavy-laden to come to him for rest. His yoke is easy and his burden is light, a sentiment that no other deity can claim. Gods of other faiths often come across as selfish and manipulative, offering nothing of eternal value. Jesus, on the other hand, welcomes those with heavy business burdens as well as personal ones, offering them respite and the opportunity for breakthrough.

Regardless of what brings you into God's presence, he relishes the opportunity to be with his child. You may think that you're burdening God with your presence, but he sees it as a chance to be with his children. He invites us to be in his presence every day, and he eagerly awaits us. He is not inconvenienced by us; on the contrary, he paid a heavy price for us because we are his inheritance. God yearns to offer you your inheritance, a poignant symbol that you are indeed His inheritance. He seeks you out, as you seek what He provides – part of which is salvation. There's nothing misguided about this pursuit. We are repeatedly guided in scripture to approach Him and no one else. God has paid the ultimate price, with His own blood, to grant us full access to His power, the power of the God of creation. Regardless of the circumstances or situations we face, we are granted access to this divine power through the blood of Jesus.

Furthermore, every word from Him is swaddled in perfect love. A unique trait is that every word from God is also wrapped in love because God is, indeed, love. This is irrefutable truth. Perfect love, as we know, casts out all fear. Any fears, worries, struggles you may experience in your life or your business, perfect love will cast them out. Love also covers a multitude of sins. Meaning, anything caused by sin is cured by love. This shift in focus requires us to endure the surprised reactions of others when we refuse to participate in their debaucheries, lawless idolatry, and the like. They may malign us for our stance, but they will have to account to God, who is ready to judge the living and the dead. We all will face judgment, and the Bible emphasizes that the blood of Jesus was poured out on our behalf to cover our sins and guilt. Through faith, we are redeemed from the curse.

While the flesh will be judged, we can live in the Spirit as God does. We're called to be self-controlled and sober minded, to continue loving one another earnestly, to show hospitality without grumbling, and to use our unique gifts to serve others as good stewards of God's grace. God never intended for us to feel separate from Him or unworthy of speaking to Him. Rather, He encourages us to walk in the supernatural grace that He has endowed us with, to serve others in our businesses and our personal lives.

In our businesses, God can make our biggest worries, struggles, and fears null and void with a single promise. When He gives you a vision for your business, He simultaneously gives you a vision for your identity. He builds you up while helping you build everything you set your hands to. God is not merely interested in your success; He is invested in building you up personally while releasing unlimited potential through you. These heavenly strategies for your business can often feel larger than what you believe you can handle. But remember, God knows you better than you know yourself. He created you, imbued you with life and bestowed you with gifts. You may have honed skills and abilities, but it was He who gave you the intelligence and capabilities to do so in the first place.

In the journey of spirituality, we must first beseech for eyes to see and ears to hear what the Spirit is communicating. However, it isn't enough to merely ask for these gifts; we must also apply our faith and truly believe that He will grant us these capabilities. Through practice, listening, and asking probing questions, we can strengthen our faith and begin to understand the strategies that the Spirit imparts. It's crucial to exercise and grow our faith, as in the face of trials and tests, our faith will provide us with steadfastness.

Reflecting on the scripture, James 1:2-8, it becomes evident that we should consider it a joy when faced with trials of any kind. The testing of our faith produces steadfastness and perfection, equipping us with completeness and the absence of lack. If we find ourselves in need of wisdom, we must turn to God in faith and without any doubt. The scripture cautions us against being double-minded and wavering in our faith, for such instability would prevent us from receiving anything from the Lord. Faith is the crux of our spiritual journey, and we must believe in it unreservedly and willingly take risks to access the strategies imparted by the Spirit. However, employing these strategies isn't enough. We must also walk in the way of the Lord, steering clear of being double-minded and avoid simultaneously following the strategies of heaven and the ways of the world.

The strategies from heaven often exceed our expectations, inducing fear due to their sheer magnitude. They might demand us to step out of our comfort zone and embrace challenges in various aspects of our lives, like business struggles, which may serve a purpose much grander than we realize. Such struggles might reveal opportunities for innovative solutions, as I experienced myself. In my struggle to market a group of people, I ended up discovering a strategy that promised a much greater increase in my business.

Walking with the Spirit demands courage and a willing heart. It's not about whether we can or can't; it's about whether we will or won't. It's never about "what if" scenarios, but rather about when "even if" circumstances arise. Our role is to rise above our doubts, believing that God works in us for His own good pleasure (Philippians 2:13). It's time to cast aside our doubts and "what if" worries, and focus on the "even if" scenarios and the decision to either act or not. Approaching God in faith for answers, we must start believing that He is for us and not against us. The judgment we receive is a form of mercy because of the blood of Jesus. We must approach Him as children, not strangers, to find answers in our time of need.

When we obtain strategies from God and implement them, our businesses could potentially outperform every competitor not led by the Spirit of God. I believe that God's current pastoral reformation and Shepherding movement will manifest in every sphere of influence and culture. Businesses led by God's Spirit can teach the world His ways, surpassing competitors, providing them with answers and teaching them His path. This journey involves teaching others the Way, consulting with the systems we surpass, leading from a place of holy conviction. It's not a matter of preference; the Kingdom is here to take over. We are here to rule. On our way to victory, we'll pass every naysayer and then offer them an opportunity to learn from us.

There's a unique mantle being released on earth at this time; a manifestation that encompasses even the Spirit of Elijah that falls on those who respond to this call. As the word speaks about Elijah, those with ears to hear should discern the significance of what I'm saying. As the crowd dispersed, Jesus turned to them and began speaking about John the Baptist, a figure of intense reverence and contemplation, a voice echoing in the wilderness, preparing the way for the Lord. "What did you expect to find in the wilderness?" He asked. "A reed swaying aimlessly in the wind? Or did you anticipate a man adorned in luxurious garments? Surely not, for such individuals reside in the opulence of royal palaces. Did you, then, set out in search of a prophet?" He continued, affirming their presumption. "Indeed, you found a prophet, but John is more than that. He is the divine messenger, preparing your way before you. Undeniably, no one born of woman is greater than John the Baptist. But the least in the kingdom of heaven is greater than he."

The dichotomy Jesus outlined here was thought-provoking. Since the advent of John the Baptist, the Kingdom of heaven has faced aggression, with forceful individuals attempting to claim it. All the prophets and the law had prophesied until John's time. And if people were open to receiving the message, they would realize that John was the embodiment of Elijah, the one prophesied to come. Jesus implored the listeners, "He who has ears to hear, let him hear."

Drawing a comparison to the current generation, Jesus depicted an image of children in marketplaces, complaining about their playmates who didn't dance when they played the flute or mourn when they sang a dirge. He highlighted the contradictory attitudes of the public towards John the Baptist, who abstained from eating and drinking and was deemed demon-possessed, and towards himself, accused of being a glutton and a drunkard, a friend of tax collectors and sinners. Regardless of the criticisms, He said, "wisdom is justified by her deeds."

We can vehemently argue and discuss the principles of the faith, but the crux of the matter remains that we are known by the fruit we bear. That is the undeniable truth that liberates us. As steadfast believers, we walk this path unflinchingly, immune to the doubts and skepticism of others. Yet, even after witnessing Jesus' miracles, some cities remained unrepentant, prompting Him to reprimand them. He declared a woe unto Korazan and Vesaida, stating that had Tyre and Sidon seen the miracles performed in these cities, they would have repented long ago. This statement serves as a stark reminder to us today. As we surpass our competitors and revolutionize industries with our God-led businesses, we will become the beacon of revival. Our achievements will bear witness to the glory of God, inspiring entire cities and industries to embrace the truth. Upon reaching such a pinnacle, we will not only be leading the industry but also guiding those who were once our competition.

Moreover, our success won't be simply about amassing wealth and influence. We will set new standards of spiritual excellence and integrity in business, bringing about transformation on a scale unimaginable. However, the journey to this pinnacle demands humility, not pride. We will be changemakers, influencing the masses, but we will do so grounded in the humility and grace bestowed on us by the Lord.

CHAPTER 5: TRICKLE FOR
TEACH, GIFT FOR INCREASE

Alright, let's dive into the 'Trickle for Teach Gift for Increase' chapter. Congratulations on making it this far; it's an accomplishment to commit to driving your business towards growth. This dedication speaks volumes about you and aligns with our shared objective. So far, we've explored a diverse range of concepts: establishing a Shepherding movement, engaging with the Holy Spirit in our business, partnering with prophets, learning to honor and communicate with the lesser. All these principles lead to one thing – increase, the subject of our discussion today. Increase, including financial increase, is a good thing. It is essential to understand that money itself is not evil; it's the love of money that corrupts. Money can be wielded as a tool, stewarded effectively to do good, or it can become an obsession that diverts your heart from God. The distinction lies in how you manage it.

As we delve deeper into the concept of Shepherding in business, we will be introduced to strategies to outperform our competitors. The goal is not only to excel but to surpass them so far that we become a resource to elevate them to higher ground. In this journey, it's crucial to stay grounded and defeat the lurking pride. A successful leader must guard against complacency and arrogance that often follow victories. It's vital to remember the fundamentals – prioritizing people, fostering communication, staying humble, and maintaining personal connections.

At times, it's necessary to remind ourselves of the value of humility. It's easy to get caught up in the exhilaration of surpassing your competitors and forget the essence of leadership – lifting others. Often, this will mean redirecting portions of your profits towards individuals and organizations that provide hope to those in need. This kind of generosity shouldn't undermine your business, although there may be occasions where you're called to give generously to break the shackles of scarcity and allow generosity to rule over money.

Here's a recent example. A local restaurant owner I met was struggling due to the COVID-19 pandemic. I suggested an idea: I would run ads for their restaurant, encouraging people to dine there with a portion of the day's proceeds going to a local organization, the Hope Center. This initiative would bring multiple benefits – increased visibility for my leadership, the restaurant, and the Hope Center, not to mention hope for the community. Despite offering to run the ads for free, the restaurant owner rejected the idea, put off by the prospect of giving money away. This reluctance overlooked the potential benefits: say the restaurant usually makes $1,000 a day. This initiative could have boosted it to $2,500. Even after donating 10% ($250), the owner would still have made $2,250, a significant increase for the day.

However, the benefits would not have been exclusively financial. The essence of this strategy lies in valuing people over profits, understanding that the former often leads to the latter. In certain situations, it might mean sacrificing potential earnings to instill lessons about compassion and generosity, which, in turn, cultivate a mindset conducive to sustainable growth.

In our journey today, we're exploring the concept of intentional suffering and how it can benefit businesses, individuals, and communities alike. One example involves an approach where businesses willingly allocate a portion of their profits to local organizations. This strategy not only aids these organizations and those they serve but can also bolster other businesses involved in the process. By creating a multi-strand network, businesses can provide a three- or even four-way opportunity that benefits themselves, their partner businesses, and the local communities they serve.

Such an approach might not seem financially profitable at first, but when viewed from a broader perspective of people and influence, it becomes clearer. This method builds trust, increases influence, and ultimately yields returns in the market, although not always financial. Some may disregard this idea as impractical, but it is a viable way to foster a culture of benevolence and communal development. As I've often found, even when initial propositions are turned down, persistence prevails. The notion is to cultivate seeds that grow into fruitful ventures, rather than mere theories or intentions.

In this context, suffering arises as a salient theme. In the case of the restaurant, for instance, the question arises: why willingly choose suffering for the benefit of others? The answer lies in understanding what suffering truly means. In our context, suffering refers to the application of pressure, much like the process of wine making. Grapes must be crushed to release their juice, which is then fermented to make wine. If the grapes aren't crushed, they'll rot, and the valuable essence within them will be lost. Similar processes can be seen in the production of oil from olives or avocados and the formation of diamonds under immense pressure.

Suffering, therefore, is not merely a state of enduring pain, distress, or hardship, but a process of transformation. It can be perceived either as an ongoing state of discomfort or as a necessary pressure that eventually yields valuable results – be it wine, oil, or diamonds. Your choice. The perspective you adopt is a crucial determinant of how you interpret and manage suffering. God placed eternity within us, enabling us to discern the course of things and fill our minds with His thoughts. We can understand His will through His Spirit, as illuminated in 1 Corinthians 2. When we allow His Spirit to reveal His thoughts, we gain a divine perspective. We can see the process of suffering for gain as a burdensome ordeal or as an opportunity to learn and grow.

Responding to suffering with a positive perspective can make a world of difference. Our mental frameworks can shape our interpretations of a situation and determine how we deal with it. Approaching suffering as an inevitable part of life that brings with it lessons and growth opportunities can help us cope with it more effectively. But in the end, the choice is ours. We can either suffer by default or decide to intentionally suffer, learn from it, and use it as a stepping stone towards our growth and development. Therefore, my recommendation is this: accept the fact that there will be situations that cause suffering, but also acknowledge that these situations can be leveraged as intentional training grounds for producing oil, wine, and diamonds in your life.

If you can firmly set your mind on the path of self-improvement and self-awareness, you won't find yourself anxiously waiting for times of suffering to descend upon you. Instead, you will actively seek out these periods of challenge and growth, choosing to immerse yourself within them. This, however, requires a certain warrior spirit - the type of individual who looks out across a battlefield and declares ownership of it. This is a person who sees obstacles and adversity, represented metaphorically as giants, and responds with unwavering faith, saying, 'God's got us. We'll take them out, no problem.'

The person it does not take is one who crumbles at the sight of these metaphorical giants, retreating in fear and succumbing to self-doubt. Those who spend their time bemoaning, whining, and griping about their situation don't make progress, as excuses rarely, if ever, lead to growth. Instead, it's the people who take action, who get things done, who make real progress. Those who wish to build a business that thrives must be prepared to face hardship and suffering. The process, however, can be rewarding and enriching in ways unimaginable.

In this context, suffering doesn't have to denote a constant state of distress, pain, and hardship. It can be interpreted as a pressing together that produces something greater - a process that turns adversity into beauty. When we actively seek guidance from the Holy Spirit, every pressing issue in our business can be met with a heavenly strategy to solve the issue. Sometimes, these strategies involve people. Yet, involving others might not always seem like a worthwhile investment at the outset. This is where the value of patience and foresight come into play. The thoughts and concepts of your heart, like seeds, need to be sown into people in order to reap a harvest. To illustrate this, let's consider a hypothetical scenario involving two individuals, Wally and

Richard.

Wally, a talented graphic designer, worked for Richard, an expert sales professional who required fifty graphics. Wally decided to offer to create the designs for $750. After completing the job, Wally felt he had undersold his work and should have charged more. In response to his grievances, the suggestion was made to approach Richard with a new deal. He knew he could probably get closer to $2000 for the graphics, but that's not what he chose to do. Instead, Wally would do another fifty graphics for the same price or less (embracing a forced suffering), on the condition that Richard taught him how to gain two new sales in his business. That was the trade, 50 more graphics for the same price, contingent upon Richard working with Wally to close two new deals in his business. Wally leaned on Richard's sales expertise, while Richard benefited from cheap design work.

This approach created more profit for Wally, cheaper design work for Richard, and both parties benefitted. This type of scenario and trade opportunity necessitates a shift from transactional relationships to transformational ones. It involves taking a hit financially for a season, in order to sow seeds into people and reap the rewards in the future. Following this principle, Wally stands to gain much more than if he had simply raised his prices and risked losing the relationship with Richard. This paradigm applies to any business, requiring one to leave behind the pursuit of immediate gain for the promise of greater benefits in the long run.

To expand on this concept, let's consider a second scenario. Imagine a coaching business owner who offers a twelve-month program for $5,000, teaching clients how to effectively coach and sell their services. Charles, a potential client, finds himself in a predicament - he feels called to leave his job to embark on an entrepreneurial venture but lacks the funds to afford the program. In response, the business owner offers to train Charles himself and give him a commission-based role in his company to cover the cost of the education and equipping.

While this decision might appear to be a loss initially,

it presents the opportunity for future growth and profit. By 'trickling for teach, and gifting for increase', or sacrificing immediate monetary gain for the chance to teach and influence a new salesperson, the business owner creates an opportunity for synergy. Charles, once trained for the sales role in the coach's business, could bring in numerous clients willing to pay the full program price. Imagine how it would feel for this coach to have blessed Charles with the equipping to launch his own coaching business, but also earning $30K in the first two months because he trained Charles to sell the $5k program in an effort to create increase while also equipping Charles to sell his own packages in the future?

In both these examples, the underlying principle is one of investment, patience, and long-term thinking. Instead of aiming for immediate gains and transactional relationships, the focus shifts towards transformational connections and the potential for greater returns in the future. Building a business around this principle might appear more challenging and time-consuming at first. However, it ultimately leads to more meaningful and fruitful collaborations, and possibly more significant business success. This principle of investing in others, teaching them, and creating synergies, reflects the spirit of unity and collective growth. It's obviously not a model one would use for every sale, every deal, or every customer interaction, but it is a dynamic way to honor the right people with the right opportunity, seemingly taking a hit at first, suffering for a little while with some extra workload, but eventually paying off as the trade begins to produce fruit.

The Bible, for instance, talks about the importance of sowing seeds (Galatians 6:7-9) and reaping a harvest in due time. It speaks of loving your neighbor as yourself (Mark 12:31) and doing to others what you would have them do to you (Matthew 7:12). So as far as the principles matter, it's in alignment with doing something good, that also produces something good.

A business that embodies these values not only stands to be more resilient and prosperous, but it also helps foster a culture of generosity, unity, and mutual growth with new prospective connections as the network grows around the change they are establishing in the earth. This kind of culture can make your business not just a money-making entity, but a force for positive change in the world. However, again, adopting this approach requires courage, faith, and a willingness to face challenges head-on. As mentioned earlier, periods of suffering can serve as catalysts for growth. And it's not always about merely enduring suffering, but embracing it, understanding that it can lead to refinement, improvement, and ultimately, success.

Remember that your business can be a platform for change, growth, and positive impact. The challenges you encounter are opportunities for growth. Adopt a long-term mindset, invest in people, and build transformational relationships. These principles can turn your business into not just a profit-making machine, but a source of blessing and positive impact for others. And most importantly, always be open to guidance from the Holy Spirit in all your decisions and endeavors. Only make these kinds of deals when it's appropriate for both parties to benefit in the long run. You're not a doormat, but you can be a springboard. Indeed, there lies an opportunity in every interaction and business decision you make. But remember, you can't seize every opportunity - it's simply not feasible nor efficient. This brings us to some of the critical principles you need to consider when navigating these waters.

As a business owner, when you opt for certain types of deals or partnerships, it's essential to ensure that they align with your business' current season and timing. You need to take into account your financial responsibility in the process, alongside agreements you've made with others, including those who are footing the bills. Your current business structure also plays a critical role. As a business owner, you wield the power to make decisions, even if they are unpopular. People may not always agree with you, but remember, it's your business, not theirs. However, while you have the liberty to do as you please, ensure your actions make financial sense for your company.

Consider the examples I've given: the restaurant owner, Wally, the graphic designer who struck a deal with Richard, and the business owner who was willing to train someone to benefit both parties. In every single one of these scenarios, all parties benefited. There was a potential financial hit (or absence) upfront, but it produced a harvest on the back end. This is the essence of my "Trickle for Teach, Give for Increase" strategy. Timing and season are critical factors. How do you gauge this? Yes, it depends on the people involved, their life stage, and what they need to develop in. But more than that, it depends on the kairos timing of the development of your company under the light of the Lord. By creating trickle to teach or give for increased opportunities, you can foster character development within your company, thus changing the game for your future by implementing some slight form of suffering that produces a greater development of integrity in your people.

If you identify a problem area within your company, creating opportunities that leverage the power of trickle for teach or give for increase can rejuvenate hope within that group. This can trigger a blessing, benefiting the entire company. However, financial feasibility might not always align with these actions. When this happens, ask for strategies to create the wealth needed to support making the deal. If you must create some cash flow before opening this kind of opportunity up for people, then do that. You're good at what you do. These types of deals should be made with wisdom, and covering the financial gap beforehand can ease the pain of the process. Just don't let that become a fear-barrier between you and the fruit of suffering.

Suppose you want to establish a trickle for teach or give for increase deal, but you can't justify the expense. If you're willing to proceed, seek the Holy Spirit for a strategy to create the income necessary to cushion the deal. Don't forsake the opportunity; instead, listen for strategy (host a roundtable), create a financial cushion, and then proceed. The importance of this action, however, goes beyond financial sense. It's about humility in business. As a business owner, you're not just running a company; you're leading people. You're setting an example that will shape your reputation and future consulting opportunities in the industry. Every action, every decision, matters: from your character to the way you treat people, to how you take care of yourself and your health. If you over-use this concept, people will begin to aim to take advantage of you. My recommendation? Keep it silent. Be a "silent investor" in the people you make these kinds of deals with. It's nobody else's business if someone can't afford your services, and the people's business you choose to help doesn't need to be advertised. You can both testify about it later if it needs to be shared, after both parties have increased and benefitted from the choice to cut this kind of deal.

Remember, building your business goes hand in hand with building your identity. You're a solutionary bringing transformative ideas to your industry. This is your purpose. Every moment, every decision, contributes to your growth.

Write this down: Anything you give time, attention, and focus to is something that can either build you or break you.

This realization might be uncomfortable, especially when you find yourself dedicating time, attention, and focus to things that don't contribute positively to your growth. These can create marks of frustration, anxiety, and anger. It's crucial to remember that your mental, emotional, and spiritual health as a business owner is of utmost importance. Anything you give your time, attention, and focus to is shaping you, so choose wisely.

In the Business I own, full of coaching, consulting, and education opportunities, one of the key principles I impart revolves around the concept of spiritual communication, particularly focusing on building influential relationships. I emphasize what I call the 'spiritual system of honor.' According to this principle, the influential voice you choose to honor is the one that shapes you in a specific season of your life. To further clarify, any voice that you consciously decide to agree with and partner with is the voice that forms a covenant with you for that particular phase. It's a concept that needs careful deliberation as you wouldn't want your emotional identity to be influenced by individuals who neither live in love nor enjoy access to personal freedom.

If those around you incite anger, frustration, hate, or focus your attention on trivial matters that aren't truly beneficial, they're fostering a negative influence. This can be especially relevant when making strategic decisions such as trickle for teach or give for increase deals in business. These opportunities demand significant time, commitment, energy, focus, and attention. Understanding this principle is crucial since the activities you invest your time and attention in inevitably contribute to your growth and development.

Applying this principle to relationships, the people we choose to invest our time, attention, and focus on also significantly contribute to our personal growth. Consequently, when faced with opportunities in business that require time, commitment, strategy, focus, and attention, it's essential to understand that these deals will shape us, not just in terms of our relationships, but also in terms of the deals themselves. For instance, even if I don't gain anything financially or relationally from helping a restaurant owner improve their business to further support a hope center, I still benefit because I am being developed.

Moreover, the question that arises is - what is being developed within us? And the answer harks back to one word - hope. Hope doesn't disappoint, and in fact, according to Romans 5:3-5, we should rejoice in our sufferings. When our businesses begin to rejoice, we should direct this jubilation towards areas of suffering. Initiating a "trickle for teach" or "give for increase" deal creates an environment of suffering, which might not sound enjoyable but bear with me. Suffering breeds endurance, which in turn fosters character and ultimately, hope. This sequence of development is profoundly meaningful for those who strive to build out a shepherding movement and grow a business that can rejoice while listening to the Holy Spirit's guidance. Embracing this principle, we understand that choosing to endure suffering, like entering into a "trickle for teach" or "give for increase" deal, instigates a process of betterment. This process manifests itself in our lives and businesses, yielding promising results.

To delve deeper, when you willingly place yourself in a position of suffering, such that the suffering gives rise to endurance; you are effectively creating emotional response longevity. This means you are cultivating resilience in your life and business, particularly concerning emotional responses. For instance, if a problem arises in your business and your immediate response is anxiety or fear, it suggests a lack of endurance. The goal is to develop a healthy emotional response to problems, cultivating resilience that promotes longevity in your life and business.

Indeed, in a "trickle for teach" or "give for increase" deal, one of the key outcomes is that it generates increased influence, trust, respect, and power among people. This strengthened relationship becomes a resource that you can tap into when needed. By entering into such a deal, you are compelled to face new challenges that demand an emotional response, thereby creating an opportunity to build stronger relationships, characterized by trust and mutual respect. I know I'm being repetitive here, maybe even redundant, but I'm trying to give you a life-hack and business-hack that will change your future for the better.

If we're genuinely committed to fostering a movement and building a business that can rejoice, and we're committed to learning to discern God's voice through various formats, we might want to consider these principles. Embracing suffering to cultivate endurance is part of this process, and this endurance will yield substantial benefits in our lives and businesses. Endurance also fosters character - a characteristic that is defined as the proven worth of someone tried and tested. This development process allows you to discover more about yourself and substantiate the qualities you've been doubting. These deals you create can serve as personal trials that refine specific aspects of your own interpersonal understanding of your own character.

This principle extends to your abilities as well. If you're uncertain about your abilities in a particular area, create a deal that allows you to test and develop that skill. The people receiving the deal are embracing an opportunity that hasn't been afforded to them previously anyway. They will be excited, if you enter into the deal a little scared. Sometimes, this might involve offering a free service that you're aiming to improve. Be transparent about your intentions, allowing the Holy Spirit to guide your development. As a result, you'll likely impress your partner, validate your abilities, and experience God's approval, all of which will boost your confidence.

Planting relational seeds along your journey can reap considerable rewards in the future. Impressing the right people can widen your network and expose you to leaders who can take you to the next level. Sometimes, being willing to assist someone can lead to unexpected opportunities, placing you in the room with influential leaders who can help shape your path. Whether it's a 'trickle for teach' or a 'give for increase' deal, embracing these principles and engaging in strategic partnerships can be a potent catalyst for personal growth and business development. The power of relationships cannot be overstated, particularly in your sphere of influence or your industry. As a leader, the relationships you cultivate with other leaders serve as the backbone for potential opportunities and a resource for wielding influence for the benefit of your people. As leaders, we often forget that we carry the ability to lead our people wherever we are willing to go. This is a principle worth reiterating - where you are willing to go, you can learn to lead your people there too.

Our journey, however, isn't devoid of trials. The Bible verse in Romans explains how suffering breeds endurance, and endurance in turn, shapes our character. This character ultimately gives birth to hope. In essence, hope is the antidote to depression. This contrast should prompt you to look closely at the characteristics of depression, as this will define what hope isn't.

As a key leader in your business and industry, you have a divine mandate to transform the world. This isn't a call to inflate your ego, but rather, a call to recognize your worth and to walk in that truth. The mindset of hope should permeate your leadership style, ruling over any seeds of depression that might arise. Hope operates on a higher realm, reigning over depression, making you an effective leader. A leader who carries hope radiates an infectious aura. This hopeful disposition provides the right words and perspective for your people, resulting in better emotional responses in all facets of life and business.

Side note: If you need help breaking mental, emotional, or spiritual strongholds, oppressions, or setbacks, I lead a team of many five-fold leaders around the world, some who may even be in your region. Reach out to me and ask for help. We've got your back.

Depression has a crippling effect on decision-making. It's important to understand this, as it could be limiting your growth potential. The moment you reject the lie that depression is your lot, you begin the journey out of that pit. Depression often stems from selfishness, self-centeredness, and self-focus. The antidote? Hope. But sometimes, to find hope, you must be willing to put in some effort, face some trials, embrace some struggles and sufferings. It's all worth it in the end if you don't give up.

The path to hope isn't easy. It involves enduring suffering to cultivate endurance, developing character, and eventually arriving at a place of hope. This process inherently gives no room for depression. The principle of 'trickle for teach' and 'give for increase', produced through revelation through Romans 5:3-5, provides an actionable plan for breaking the stronghold of depression in your business. Ready to end your business's depression? Follow this concept and ask the Holy Spirit for instruction on how to implement it. Host a roundtable. Invite real prophets.

Leading a business that successfully develops people and propounds the best strategies requires shepherding skills. However, shepherding doesn't mean isolating yourself in a corner, afraid of exposing your identity to your community and industry. You were not born to think that way. Leading effectively involves carrying responsibilities that not many people understand or are skilled enough to accomplish. One of these responsibilities involves actively seeking out and eradicating depression within your people.

Yes, the responsibility extends even to their families.

Sometimes, you may have to engage with the families of your staff, employees, service providers, and even your competitors. You may not be a therapist or a mental health counselor, but as a leader, you can still cultivate an environment of hope. The decisions you make as a leader can inspire hope by allowing people to endure suffering, develop character, and find hope. This process inherently breaks the stronghold of depression, providing a healthier and more productive environment for everyone involved.

If an opportunity arises for you to make a 'trickle for teach' or 'give for increase' deal, consider the benefits it can bring not only to you but to those around you. Reflect on the importance of emotional health as the leader of your business, and recognize the power you wield to instill hope in your people through the deals you make. This realization may evoke a sense of responsibility, joy, or even awe. Remember, as a leader, you hold the key to a hopeful and productive environment, making decisions that can change lives for the better.

CHAPTER 6: BUILDING A PEOPLE, RELEASING THE KINGDOM

We are now at the sixth chapter of our "Teach your Business to Rejoice." As we reflect on the past sessions, we have covered a lot of ground. In our first session, we talked about the power of pure communication and the importance of presence in building trust. We discussed how trust is a bank account where deposits and withdrawals are made, granting us access to an inheritance of relationships and opportunities. In session two, we talked about the art of impression, and how involving the right people in your business can create a lasting imprint based on the Creator's design. Session three touched on the importance of bestowing greater honor on the seemingly least important aspects of our business - whether that's people or products. In recognizing their value, all members of the business can rejoice. Session four delved into the need for a strategy in every facet of your business. We discussed the ways to seek divine guidance and insights for business problems. Following this, session five introduced the principle of "trickle for teach" and "give for increase", illustrating the importance of endurance, character, and hope in crushing the presence of depression in your business.

In this session, we turn our attention to a different concept, one that might seem counter intuitive. Rather than focusing on building systems and fitting people into them, we should focus on building people. This is a principle that God revealed to me. He said, "Don't build systems and fill them with people. Build a people, and I will establish the kingdom through them."

The world, without eternal divine intelligence, tends to create systems and populate them with people, teaching others to do the same. However, God, the Creator of the universe, originally established a perfect system of honor when he gave man dominion over the earth. This divine system was marred when man chose to sin, resulting in a curse that has led mankind to struggle, toil, and labor ever since. We often see people creating systems or models as a result of their struggle, finding formulas and methods that work to mitigate the impact of the curse. However, if we align ourselves with God's original design, we can partner with something truly powerful. God, the Creator of all, knows how to build something that can change everything. If there's any model or system you want to follow, it should be God's. He is always right and never lies.

However, let the one who has ears hear what the Spirit is saying. Man builds systems and then fills them with people, but God builds people and releases the Kingdom through them. He established the Church not on the foundation of apostolic and prophetic principles with Christian systems as the cornerstone, but on the foundation of apostles and prophets, with Christ as the cornerstone. When we build our businesses on people, we get kingdom results. We should ask ourselves: "Should we build our businesses like God builds His kingdom?" We can choose to build things the way they're intended to be built or not, to love and shepherd people like the Creator does or not. But remember, having a heart to build a people instead of systems isn't normal. It requires eternal conversations and divine strategies.

When we let the Spirit move freely in our businesses, supernatural power becomes present. However, when we fail to partner with God and get eternal strategies, we end up off track, out of alignment, confused, and fearful. In your business, do you feel out of alignment or confused? Are you worried about how things are going? When you're in conversation and community with God, you create a covenant that protects your business and provides divine strategies. The alternative is to ignore these divine conversations and miss the opportunity for divine intervention in your business.

But this was never God's goal for his kingdom, nor for leadership. According to the verse in 1 John 2:27, "And you no longer have need for a teacher because the anointing that abides in you will teach you all things." The Holy Spirit was sent to instruct us in all things, not just some. However, many have never heeded the Holy Spirit and are largely unfamiliar with His true nature. They presume that the Holy Spirit is simply a mouthpiece for faith-based, right-wing, evangelical Christianity. This misrepresentation in the US of God's heart comes from those pretending to hear Him while simultaneously neglecting and ignoring Him. The Father isn't a political ruler. Jesus isn't a democrat or republican, He is the King of kings.

Teachers still hold importance in our growth and journey within the kingdom. However, their role isn't to dictate how things should be done. A true God-anointed teacher will guide you on how to form a partnership with God in everything you do. The best teachers will show you how to get answers and strategies from God, allowing you to operate independently, leaning on the guidance of the Holy Spirit within you.

So now, we must ask ourselves, do we have a good teacher in our lives? And by that, I don't mean someone who can teach us a few things about business or life, but someone who can guide us into a divine conversation with God. As a teacher, my role is not to provide you with strategies, but to guide you towards a deeper relationship with God and His wisdom, outlining this knowledge in the form of a book that encourages an ongoing dialogue with the Creator of the universe.

As we engage more in conversation with God, our love for people will grow, reflecting God's own love. We are made in God's image, and the more we spend time with Him, the more His character, integrity, and identity manifest within us. Jesus demonstrated this principle by only saying and doing what He perceived the Father saying and doing. We must strive for this level of spiritual communion and impartation. My own journey in this respect is ongoing, and while I feel I'm drawing closer, I know there is still much room for growth. However, I am committed to continuous growth and moving ever closer to this ideal. The departure from the old way of being is certainly complete, and now it's all about the journey towards arrival at each moment He has destined for me to encounter in His will.

As an apostle within the Kingdom of God, my sphere of influence is often within religious circles first, but transcends that sphere and moves into the dominion my true calling, to activate leaders regardless of industry. As a transitional apostle, my mission is to lead by example, bringing a fresh light on the Kingdom to the church. I am committed to fostering reform and transformation in how churches lead people. Currently, I see significant issues with church operations, which are contrary to the provisions that God has given to the church. It's not hard to recognize that the church is prominently deceived and following traditionally broken ways of operation, leading to dead churches, dry movements, and minimal impact. That's not the influence of my Father. It's the influence of the devil. This raises a vital point on the difference between influence and intentionality. If you sow a seed into the field of intentionality, it will yield influence. However, sowing a seed into influence will not result in intentionality, instead producing a falsity that, while pleasing to the eye, is not authentic. The means to gaining influence must be by nurturing a field of intentionality, not by seeking influence directly. Hence, your strategy must be unique to your mandate, guided by the Holy Spirit, not mimicked from others, whether it's a church or a business.

Most churches are failing because they follow a broken model that literally leads to producing broken leaders of empty buildings. Sadly, most people within the church, within my sphere of influence, are not being adequately shepherded, which should be the primary goal of our religious community. Even leaders need shepherds. Many individuals within a religious community may be receiving weekly teachings or sugar coated 20-minute pep talks, depending on their leadership, but most of them lack personal relationships with their pastors. In essence, pastors are supposed to be shepherds, yet the absence of personal relationships between parishioners and their leaders is a stark deviation from the biblical teachings. John 10:27 states, "my sheep hear me. I know them, they follow me." This suggests that the sheep, or the followers, should have a deep familiarity with the voice of their shepherd, or pastor.

As I've reached thousands around the world with opportunities to advance in ministry and leadership, I ask questions I've developed. I'll ask, "Do you go to church?" They'll respond, "Yes." I'll ask, "Great! Who is your pastor?" They respond "Brother or Sister 'so and so'." Then, I say, "When is the last time that they have actually called you or met with you in person to talk about your life, the warfare you deal with, your family dynamics and needs, etc.?"

The response, 98% of the time? "I've never experienced that call or conversation."

Regrettably, the pursuit of influence often leads many away from the Biblical model of true leadership. If the goal is merely to disseminate a message, systems might be sufficient. However, if the intention is to genuinely shepherd people—to guide and support them personally—then the focus needs to be on individual relationships rather than systems. Tragically, the trap that many leaders fall into is that they start with the intention to shepherd people, but as soon as a system appears to work, the focus shifts to shepherding the system. This is a form of double-mindedness, setting out with one intention, but not sowing the seeds required to bring that intention to fruition. Loving a system, but neglecting the people the system was built to bring in.

For pastors to truly shepherd, they must be in relationship with their flock. Therefore some (most) churches are empty - their leaders aren't connecting with every member, they're not shepherding everyone. And while it may be unrealistic to expect one pastor to personally shepherd hundreds of people, God didn't expect that either, which is why he equips many pastors. The model given in Scripture is a five-fold model that makes room and leaders for literally every person, with no excuse to leave anyone unattended to. I'll fight the liars on that until I die.

However, the prevailing business models don't always support this multi-shepherd concept, either. This calls for a critical reevaluation of these models. If the system being built can't operate in the way that God intended for influence to flourish, changes are necessary. Business-minded leaders who've earned degrees and certifications in managing systems often get hired as pastors. Yet instead of working within a divinely inspired model that focuses on personal relationships, these pastors end up managing systems, not people. This often leads to unfulfillment, stagnating growth, empty churches, and barely profitable businesses.

As a business owner, what if you could lead your people in a way that expresses the fullness of supernatural favor and alignment with the Word of God, teaching churches what shepherding actually looks like? Wow... that might be weird to you. Or it might give you a challenge worth accepting. What if the church will actually be corrected by business leaders who teach and steward a better way until the pastors ask us how we're leading so many people effectively? These issues aren't confined to the church; they also pervade all forms of business. To create a thriving business that brings joy to those involved, leaders must embrace a new paradigm. The principles of focusing on people over systems are not simply ideas, concepts, or theories I've devised. They are based on the divine blueprint provided by our Creator. Instead of building a system and filling it with people, we should build people, who can then experience the power of God when he moves to create an unlimited number of systems through the people you're willing to raise up.

When the Holy Spirit was poured out on all flesh, as described in Acts Chapter 2, it sparked a wildfire of faith. Implementing a people-first, God-inspired approach to life. In your business, this is akin to sparking such a wildfire. While the initial effort may seem small—a mere spark—it can ignite a blaze that rapidly expands. This isn't a nuclear explosion; it moves and spreads organically, like a wildfire. We are in a torch race, each person who carries their spiritual fire is meant to pass it on, igniting others. This passing of the torch of reassurance must happen through people, not systems. Systems can't be encouraged to operate in the supernatural, but people can. When people are ignited by the divine fire, they can hear from God and release His wisdom to the world.

Lastly, we must remember that systems can't prophesy or anticipate new things. Amos 3:7 states, "God does no new thing without first revealing his secret to his servants, the prophets." Systems can't recognize these divine secrets, and they can't detect when the people within them become negative or sluggish. They lack the capability to operate in divine wisdom and knowledge, and they certainly can't operate in spiritual gifts. Only people can. This is why it's time to ignite people, to bring light into the world.

People are astute observers. They can detect when others become negative and sluggish, or when they need a new strategy or rejuvenation. This highlights the immense power vested in people, a power that God Himself has imbued in us. This power is the focal point of our discussion today. Deuteronomy 8:18 refers to it, stating that we've been given the power to create wealth. Yet, while many would use this to tell people to get money hungry on God's watch, let me give you the full Scripture.

Deuteronomy 8:11-20 ESV "Take care lest you forget the Lord your God by not keeping his commandments and his rules and his statutes, which I command you today, 12 lest, when you have eaten and are full and have built good houses and live in them, 13 and when your herds and flocks multiply and your silver and gold is multiplied and all that you have is multiplied, 14 then your heart be lifted up, and you forget the Lord your God, who brought you out of the land of Egypt, out of the house of slavery, 15 who led you through the great and terrifying wilderness, with its fiery serpents and scorpions and thirsty ground where there was no water, who brought you water out of the flinty rock, 16 who fed you in the wilderness with manna that your fathers did not know, that he might humble you and test you, to do you good in the end. 17 Beware lest you say in your heart, 'My power and the might of my hand have gotten me this wealth.' 18 You shall remember the Lord your God, for it is he who gives you power to get wealth, that he may confirm his covenant that he swore to your fathers, as it is this day. 19 And if you forget the Lord your

God and go after other gods and serve them and worship them, I solemnly warn you today that you shall surely perish. 20 Like the nations that the Lord makes to perish before you, so shall you perish because you would not obey the voice of the Lord your God."

But what does this power mean, and how can one harness it? In exploring this concept of power as depicted in scripture, we encounter the Greek word "dunamis" (D-Y-N-A-M-I-S), which means strength, power, and ability. This ability is the same that was mentioned in the parable where a master distributed money to his servants, each according to their capability. This God-given power yields an ability within you that you might not have believed was possible. It is an inherent power, which is part of your inheritance. It descends upon you when you listen to God. The power is present in a thing by virtue of its nature, much like when God speaks to you and you recognize yourself as a child of God. He then fathers you, with the Greek definition of "father" being "one who infuses his spirit into his offspring for the purpose of actuating and governing the mind."

This power is exerted or put forth in various ways, such as healing the sick, raising the dead, or even changing the world in some other way. This power is released through you into whatever your hands touch. Following Jesus' ascension, he sent the Holy Spirit, promising us that we would perform miracles just as He did, and even greater ones.

The term "dunamis" encapsulates more than just the ability to perform miracles; it also includes moral power and the excellence of the soul. It's the power that helps you maintain a sound mind, stay focused, and avoid distractions, anxiety, or depression. It enables you to make the right decisions and act excellently, which fosters influence. The influence that comes with riches and wealth is also included in the definition of "dunamis." Dunamis is not only the power and ability associated with wealth and riches but also the power and resources arising from numbers. This could pertain to numerical finances or groups of people. Moreover, "dunamis" signifies power consisting of or resting upon armies, forces, and hosts. As I mentioned earlier in this course, you are a king or a queen, and it is now time to build your army.

Your army is composed of people who fight on your behalf and defend what you're striving for. As a leader of this generation, understand that you have an army to build. The most effective armies have always operated by releasing power, intelligence, and strategy through their people, who then effectively remove problems and provide solutions. In essence, if you want to operate in power, you must learn to shepherd and move in the power of God, the power He manifests through people. This isn't about constructing a business with rigid systems and models. Instead, it's about nurturing people and allowing organic models, systems, and structures to evolve from them.

As people change and evolve, your systems and models should adapt accordingly. Doing this creates room for growth and progress. God releases power through or for people, not through or for systems. If we build something and anticipate that God will fill it with His power, like some mechanical or technological contraption, we're approaching it the wrong way. Instead, we should look at it from the perspective of God building us as He gives us divine strategy. He doesn't allow you to empower a system. Instead, to alter a system's abilities, God bestows wisdom on people, who then make the necessary adjustments that unlock the miraculous. Systems, devoid of people, are simply machines. So, to truly tap into divine power, we must focus on fostering the potential of people, not systems.

Think seriously about this - what if you die? What will happen to the works of your hands? If what you're doing right now is solo, building systems that allow you to operate your business by yourself, what happens when you're gone? Who will take over? If something happens, have you really changed the world, or did you merely come close to building something of substance? It's a heavy question, but it's time to contemplate legacy. Proverbs 13:22 states, "A good man leaves an inheritance to his children's children."

What you're building, what you're releasing, what you're called to do on Earth, it isn't just for you. You're not here just to make ends meet, pay your bills, and get by, or to provide a little while you're here. You're here to construct something that will bless not only your children but also your children's children. Perhaps you don't have children yet. In that case, what you're building should influence not only the next generation but two generations down the line.

Being a good leader requires foresight. What I'm constructing as a leader is a legacy. If I were to die today, my work would continue because the people around me would carry it forward. I am leaving an inheritance for my children, creating opportunities for all those involved, their children, and even their children's children. When you bring people into your team, you're not just inviting individuals; you're incorporating families. You're choosing to bless multiple generations within those families. Have you ever considered that you, as a leader, have a responsibility to shepherd and establish kingdom principles? This responsibility helps everyone involved in your business to construct a memorable legacy and leave an inheritance for their children's children.

Leaving an inheritance isn't just about money; it also involves the legacy you leave behind through your character, your integrity, and how you honor and treat people. My football coach used to ask, "How do you want to be remembered?" This question wasn't just important for me but for the entire team. It made us consider how we wanted our efforts to be recalled. This notion stuck with me, and I carry it into every season of my life and every project that I undertake.

Jesus left such a legacy that even after 2000 years, people still write books about him. There were so many works of Jesus that not all could be documented - a testament to his impactful legacy.

Psalm 112, verses one through three, highlights the blessings that come from fearing the Lord and delighting in his commandments. The scripture promises that those who follow this path will have mighty offspring, and the generations of the upright will be blessed. It further states, "Wealth and riches are in his house, and his righteousness endures forever."

To ensure this increase, it's necessary to build people well and to communicate with the Creator. It's impossible to speak with God and not begin to love and follow him. God is good; there's nothing evil in him. He never lies, never leaves, never forsakes, but forgives. He built us to create and release something extraordinary, which is our calling. We're not here to follow the models everyone else has built or create our own models and then try to force people into them. Instead, our calling is to build people, not just systems. Empty churches, sadly, offer a pertinent example. Despite their present state, they often espouse a model that does not focus on building people. We need to remedy this situation, offering a new approach to fulfill our true calling.

Often, solutions arrive hand-in-hand with confrontation. Many churches stand empty today, yet a phrase often heard is, "Let's get you plugged in." Plugged into what, exactly? Are you connecting me to a system that may be detrimental to individuals and bereft of kingdom solutions? Or are you integrating me into a community in pursuit of the Father? These questions are essential, as we need to understand that it doesn't have to be this way.

What if, instead of frequent turnovers and people departing, you actually shepherded them? What if, in times of their non-performance, you nurtured them rather than severing the connection? People can be challenging, but overcoming these challenges to aid them is the essence of shepherding. At times, it involves employing the metaphorical rod and staff. This allegory refers to a shepherd breaking the leg of a straying sheep to prevent it from running away. But the shepherd doesn't just inflict the injury and leave; he tends to the wound, cares for the sheep, defends it from harm, and oversees its recovery process. That's what it truly means to shepherd. If the response to a struggling individual is swift termination, that is not shepherding.

The willingness to build people is imperative. If we embrace this approach, God will release unlimited systems through them, Kingdom principles, and endless possibilities. This topic marks the conclusion of our sixth session. Now, let's move towards the homework questions.

    1. Should we build our businesses like God builds his kingdom? If your answer is yes or no, explain your reasoning.

    2. Are you willing to alter your models and structures to better steward a shepherding movement? Why or why not?

These two questions form the core of this chapter's homework. Hopefully, this session has encouraged you and provided some key insights. Our next and final chapter, chapter seven, will address how to confront the naysayers. Let's get into it!

CHAPTER 7: GO TELL THAT FOX!

Welcome to the final chapter of 'Teach Your Business to Rejoice!' If you've made it this far, having watched all the previous videos, then congratulations. You're on the final stretch, which is quite an achievement. This chapter, aptly named 'Go Tell That Fox,' will guide us on how to silence our detractors while we pursue our path to success. The first thing I'd like to emphasize is to 'just do it.' Once you start receiving divine strategies for your business and life, don't hesitate. Act on them. Remember, obeying the Holy Spirit's strategies will never lead you astray. So, don't be afraid to make the leap and 'just do it.' This advice may sound trivial, but it's necessary considering the number of naysayers you'll encounter along your journey.

People might think you're crazy for saying yes to God, or question your decisions, but remember, greatness never emerges from comfort zones. You might be called names like 'uncoachable,' 'unteachable,' 'rebel,' or 'maverick.' When people warn others about you, tell them to go fly a kite and then continue obeying the Holy Spirit's strategies. It's crucial not to allow people who stir up quarrels, drama, or fights to derail your progress. Remove drama from your life; you will observe the peace it brings. Don't tolerate adults behaving like children and causing unnecessary strife.

Strive to maintain a high-level conversation and establish it as your new norm. Walking in your inheritance isn't a one-time experience; it's a continual journey, an 'all-time experience.' Don't allow people to defer your hope because deferred hope makes the heart sick. Continue to shepherd and care for people, but when quarrels persist, put your foot down and distance yourself from people who aren't committed to the vision of the Holy Spirit for your business.

When Jesus was on Earth, people constantly stirred him up. They contested with him, bringing arguments, fights, and accusations because he was going against the grain. He obeyed his Father, which made people uncomfortable as he was outside their control and jurisdiction. You may face similar naysayers when you start following God's strategies for your business. The manifestation of these battles is spiritual warfare. The wars we face often come through people, instigating unnecessary spiritual battles. Life and death lie in the power of the tongue, and people create problems by running their mouths at each other. Remember

Luke 13:32, one of my favorite verses from the Bible. "And he said to them, "Go and tell that fox, 'Behold, I cast out demons and perform cures today and tomorrow, and the third day I finish my course."

We will dive deeper into it later in this session. But before we do that, I want to share a few stories from my life, stories about leading, facing naysayers, moving forward, and finally attaining freedom and breakthrough. Some of these might sound familiar, but listen from a leader's perspective who told naysayers to shut up and kept moving forward.

I would like to invite you to view things from a certain perspective and consider what these stories might mean for you, how they might relate to your life, and how you operate. The first tale I want to share transpired just a few weeks ago. In our school, within our coaching program, we had a woman who was training to become a coach, which is a common occurrence in this program. Unfortunately, she contracted COVID-19, an ordeal that lasted for approximately three weeks. This took place as she was entering King's company and her health was significantly compromised.

After a grueling battle with the virus, she finally recovered, and then had made the decision to get vaccinated as she planned to embark on mission trips. The destination she was traveling to required vaccination. After seeking divine guidance, she got vaccinated. However, the Delta variant of the virus soon struck her, rendering her helpless once again. In that situation, I felt a divine command to lay my hands on her and rid her body of the virus. My immediate thought was of public perception, as I intended to visit her without wearing a mask, which is a choice I consciously made. I decided to not only go to her place but also take my kids and wife along, believing firmly in the divine protection that guarded us.

Some people might call this action ignorant or risky, but I was confident that no harm would come to us. The reasoning behind this was a deep-seated belief in the sanctity of our bodies, considering them as holy grounds where no harmful seed could grow. Thus, I rejected worldly fears, listened to the Holy Spirit, and acted accordingly. Despite driving for five hours, we reached her place where she was wearing a mask. I asked her to remove it. With my family in tow, we entered her house, laid hands on her, prayed for her recovery and declared her body as holy ground. Immediately, she transformed from a woman who struggled to dress due to her difficulty in breathing, to one who was healed in an instant. A subsequent COVID-19 test confirmed her healing within 30 minutes of me laying hands.

In order to bring about this miraculous change, I had to discard negative voices, naysayers, and even doubts within my mind that stood against God's instruction. I chose not to entertain arguments that accused me of putting my family at risk; instead, I firmly believed that we were exposing the virus to the truth. And indeed, we were all safe and healthy. Obeying divine guidance paved the way for supernatural intervention.

Let me share another story from around seven years ago. Until that time, I had never taught from the Bible to a group. A small group which we were part of had to move their meetings to our house. I asked for divine guidance about what I should teach, and was led to the Book of Daniel. After two weeks of teaching from the first three chapters of Daniel, which talk about dreams and their interpretation, we had interpreted 23 dreams that were revelatory for people in our group. Our group started growing exponentially, drawing people from different churches in the region. The growth of our group caught the attention of a local church's small group pastor who wanted to meet me. He was curious about what I was teaching that was causing such an expansion. When I shared that I was teaching from the Book of Daniel, he rebuffed me saying I wasn't qualified or certified to teach the Bible. His claim seemed 'logical,' but was not rooted in biblical teachings. His inability to control me seemed to anger him. However, I told him in no uncertain terms that I would follow the instructions of the Holy Spirit and that their church's norms would not dictate my actions. Thus, the group continued to grow, with one meeting even having 33 attendees moving in their spiritual gifts and being delivered of demonic forces.

In this packed setting, we experienced numerous divine interventions. People were delivered from their struggles; miraculous healings took place including a paralyzed arm regaining full functionality, bodies being healed, and many more. Through this, I realized that throughout life, there would be people who would reject my actions. Jesus faced similar pushback. People constantly told him not to perform his actions, questioning his qualifications. However, obedience to divine guidance can provoke resistance, and it's up to others to deal with it.

In your journey of obedience and faith, it is inevitable that you will encounter resistance. There will be people who misunderstand your actions and question your motives. They'll throw their words at you and voice their doubts. But remember, it's not your business what they think of you. It's crucial to maintain your focus on your obedience to the divine call. This is what truly matters.

Let me share an instance from the time I was building the King's Company. I was running a class called 'SG&A,' a spiritual gifts identifier and activations program. Concurrently, we also offered book publishing services. Predictably, a call came from another social influencer who questioned my competence, saying I was unqualified. I replied firmly, telling them metaphorically to "go fly a kite." We proceeded anyway and ended up publishing many of our coaches' books due to our obedience to our calling.

This experience led to a fascinating revelation - once people started operating in their spiritual gifts and creating content, things began to flourish. This gave me a vision of how to build the next part of my business. We chose to prioritize obedience to the Holy Spirit and strived for excellence, and it led to tangible results and growth.

Following this, we ran something called the 'Five-fold Challenge.' A little background for those not familiar with church terminology: globally, out of those who identify as Christian, 20% of the global church, approximately 640 million people, would claim to be charismatic. These are believers who maintain they can hear God's voice. The other 80%, however, seem to be charting their own course. They don't believe they can hear His voice, hence they don't listen. They follow their own logical path instead of seeking divine strategies. In launching the Fivefold Challenge, I faced resistance from those who didn't believe in spiritual gifts or that the Holy Spirit communicates with us. Many leaders in the church questioned my identity and abilities. In response, I had to again stand firm in my faith and tell those naysayers to "go fly a kite."

Fast forward to the present day, I'm teaching business owners, most of whom are older than me, how to establish a shepherding movement in their business. I know the naysayers are still around, but I'm undeterred. I believe in the vision God has shown me. I'm aware that there will always be naysayers - those who see what we're doing and choose not to believe in it. But their disbelief does not sway me. I am unwavering in my pursuit of teaching and establishing shepherding movements in every industry in the world by obeying the voice of God. In every step of my journey, there were voices saying, "You can't do this." They predicted the demise of TKC, but we've continued to prove them wrong. Their words didn't fizzle out our determination. We're here, and we're moving forward, and there's nothing that's going to stop us. My business rejoices, and there's nothing that's going to keep me from teaching others to do so as I teach it to do so. I don't allow negative emotions or thoughts to affect my life. Those fiery darts of the enemy get blocked by my shield of faith. The devil loses, every time.

I'm not saying this out of pride, but stating the facts as they are. This is the Kingdom, and we're here to rule. One day, the sky is going to crack, and every knee will bow, every tongue will confess that Jesus is Lord. These are the facts, and this is the reality we stand on.

Here's what transpired. The Pharisees, the tradition-bound, unbelieving believers who believe they understand God better than God himself, came to Jesus. These individuals had been opposing God with their pride-filled, pious religion, building systems and models that acted as stumbling blocks for God's people. They were the same ones stumbling over themselves, striving to be heard and seen in their religious pretense. But they met the true Jesus, and their identities flourished as He identified them and made known to them their true purpose. When Pharisees approached Jesus, they warned him to flee, for Herod sought his life. In my own life, I've had similar encounters with individuals suggesting I abandon my endeavors, saying they wouldn't work, even insinuating that danger lurked around the corner. Jesus, however, had a message for these fraudsters. He responded, "Go tell that fox, behold, I cast out demons and perform cures today and tomorrow, and on the third day, I'll finish my course." In the same way He responded to Herod, you should respond to everyone who combats what you hear from the Holy Spirit, confirmed by prophets.

Let's step back a bit. At that hour, these Pharisees, these impostors, these tradition-clinging losers came to him with their warning, and Jesus's response was firm and confident. He'd continue doing what he was called to do, what his father had instructed him to do. That's the essence of God, a man of war. That's Jesus, the Messiah. When you obey the Holy Spirit, understand that you are right. The act of obedience gives you the confidence to walk boldly as a Kingdom ambassador with a thriving business. This is about establishing Kingdom principles in your business, about partnering with the voice of the Holy Spirit, and learning to hear Him. It involves collaborating with

God's people, like prophetic business consultants, learning to equip your people to derive strategies and answers directly from God.

It's about solutionary rooms, about visionaries, and about the incredible things that can be produced through people. It's about understanding the art of impression and how God designs us through each other's expressions. There's enormous power in what you can achieve with people. Learn the principles that will enable you to grow and lead a movement on Earth. I promise that you will never be sorry for obeying the Holy Spirit, even when people whine about what you're doing and how it inflicts destruction upon their limited systems..

As we reach the end of chapter seven, and the end of this book, I hope these teachings have resonated with you. My intention moving forward is to engage with those who are truly ready to embrace these concepts and take the next step. I must stress, I'm only interested in working with those genuinely committed to this journey. I have no desire to waste either your time or mine on half-hearted efforts.

A Personal Letter From The Author:

The next phase of this journey involves a one-on-one discussion about your future and the future of your business. This isn't just about you as a leader, but also about your business as a separate entity. This season of my life sees God enabling me to partner with people, and their businesses, in a bid to create something truly remarkable. In the past, my focus was largely on individuals, but now I'm excited to extend that partnership to include individuals positioned to lead God-inspired businesses too.

This invitation to a conversation is significant for both of us. It concerns you as a leader of your business, and me as an apostle in the Kingdom of heaven. I firmly believe it's time for me to partner with some business owners to enact real change in the world, and I'm prepared to step up to the challenge. I'm already working with many leaders who are experiencing exponential results in their lives and businesses. If you feel connected to the teachings

I've shared and believe they can be applied effectively in your own endeavors, then I'd like to speak with you.

Yes, there will be an offer made during the call, but rest assured, I'm open to flexible deals and arrangements. I'm about to give my email address to contact me.

Whether your business is non-existent, a startup, a small venture with a handful of employees, or an established company with a large workforce, I want to hear from you. If you provide B2B services, are a social influencer, a course creator, operate an online or brick-and-mortar business, I'm interested in helping you, but we need to have a conversation. If you're serious about creating something impactful with my assistance, then let's discuss that.

My email is tyler@thekingscompany-creations.com

Now, to the homework question for this chapter:

1. *Why is it important to obey God over the voice of your enemies? This question may be singular, but I want you to delve deep.*

2. *Explain the significance of choosing obedience to God's voice over that of your enemies.*

Once you've thought this through, email me. This connection is an opportunity to establish a shepherding movement in your business, to apply these principles, and to elevate your life to the next level. So, with that in mind, I'll leave you to reflect on this question and consider whether you're ready to take the next step. I look forward to speaking with those ready to move forward. Until then, take care, and thanks for reading this book. I trust that it has been a blessing for you, and I want to be honest. I don't want this journey to end here. I want to help you build. All you need to do is contact me through the email above. If not, I guess that's fine... but it's not ideal. I'd rather help you make significant waves in your industry and in the advancement of your movement.

Let's shake nations together!

- Apostle Tyler Frick

ABOUT THE AUTHOR

Tyler Frick

Apostle Tyler Frick is husband and a father of four boys. He is the Founder of The King's Company, a global ministry that raises up Kingdom Ministers, Coaches, and Five-Fold Leaders. He is a pioneer and trailblazer dedicated to raising up Kingdom-minded leaders for ministry, business, and creativity. His focus is to raise up leaders in the body of Christ to walk in the fullness of their five-fold ministries. He does this by  overseeing a team of leaders who coach and equip leaders around the world through the "Kingdom Life Coaching School" at The King's Company. The school provides education and coaching created to meet some of the most critical needs in the body of Christ, including Freedom from Mental & Emotional Chaos, Understanding Spiritual Warfare, Leading with Prophetic Accuracy & Stewardship, Kingdom Finances, Healthy Deliverance Ministry, equipping believers in their Gifts, Callings, Mandates, and more!

In addition to leading The King's Company's efforts to raise up Ministers and Kingdom Life Coaches, he also serves other pioneers in dynamic one on one relationships as a Business

Consultant. He helps those called to lead Kingdom Movements through Coaching, Education, and LIVE Events establish and scale their ministries, businesses, and movements with online systems and dynamic approaches to influence and impact for the Gospel.

www.ingramcontent.com/pod-product-compliance
Lightning Source LLC
Chambersburg PA
CBHW060852220526
45466CB00003B/1344